Basic
Stairbuilding

SCOTT SCHUTTNER

The Taunton Press

Photos: Deborah Fillion, Jim Hall, Paul Bertorelli, and Scott Phillips

Printed in the United States of America
10 9 8 7 6

For Pros / By Pros®: Basic Stairbuilding
was originally published in 1990 by
The Taunton Press, Inc.

For Pros / By Pros® is a trademark of The Taunton Press, Inc.,
registered in the U.S. Patent and Trademark Office.

The Taunton Press, Inc., 63 South Main Street,
PO Box 5506, Newtown, CT 06470-5506
e-mail: tp@taunton.com

The Taunton Press
Inspiration for hands-on living™

Library of Congress Cataloging-in-Publication Data

Schuttner, Scott, 1947 - .
    For Pros / By Pros®: Basic stairbuilding /
Scott Schuttner.
        p.   cm.
    Includes index.
    ISBN 1-56158-322-7
    1. Basic stairbuilding. — I. Title.
TH5695.S29   1998   89-50517
694'.6 — dc20   CIP

This book is dedicated to my wife, Glynn Hoener, and our children, Silvan and Linnaea.

Contents

Introduction

Why should anyone want to learn how to build a set of stairs? If you're a carpenter the answer is obvious. Although there's plenty of specialization in construction, stairbuilding still falls squarely into the carpenter's bag of tricks. Most houses have at least one stair and many have two or more, so sooner or later, every carpenter has to build one. If you're an owner-builder, tackling a set of stairs might be a matter of saving money, a concern for first-rate quality or the simple satisfaction of building one of the most complex parts of a house.

Stairbuilding is often thought of as being beyond the ability of the average person, but I don't believe this is true. If you've managed to build the house in the first place or complete an extensive remodel, then the stairway will be just one more detail requiring a little extra study and planning. But where should you go for that information? When I became a carpenter in the early 1970s, there were only one or two decent manuals on stairbuilding, and because these lumped simple stairs with more advanced work, they sacrificed depth for breadth. The crafts revival of the mid-1970s gave us many good books on rediscovered trades, but somehow no good text on basic stairbuilding found its way into print. I hope that this book—and the video that accompanies it—will fill the need for information on basic stairwork.

About this book. Having learned the stair trade largely from research and experience, I have concluded that the best way to teach stairbuilding is to explain the principles, rather than attempting to offer an example for every situation you might encounter. In both the book and the video, I show how to build two kinds of stairs, a straight case and an L-shaped case for tight quarters. Two construction methods are illustrated: carpeted treads and hardwood treads. In my opinion, carpeted stairs have great appeal. They're quiet and padded enough for kids to play on safely. Because the woodwork will be covered, a carpeted stair is a good choice for the first-time stairbuilder. More ambitious readers may want to attempt an elaborate oak staircase, whose beauty may become the centerpiece of the house.

The tape is complete enough to stand on its own, but the book offers valuable detail on both types of stairs, and also includes a short chapter on an open-riser ladder stair. I picked these three stairs because they illustrate enough stairbuilding fundamentals to allow you to apply what you've learned to your particular job. This is not to say that you won't have to seek additional information on different styles or details, but I hope you won't continually be searching the book for "your stairs." The book and tape are meant to be complementary. Because it proved impractical to discuss some details on camera, the tape displays specific page references where additional information can be found in the book.

Tools, materials and costs. Building a staircase can be simple or complicated, depending on its size, the design and the materials you pick. In any case, no special tools are required beyond a good complement of hand woodworking tools, plus a circular saw, a router and a drill. A table saw will prove valuable too, although it isn't absolutely necessary. You'll need a good assortment of bits, fasteners and clamps as well. As is evident from the tape, the work is best done on site, right in the house, so be prepared to put up with the mess for a while.

As construction work goes, stairs are relatively material intensive and labor intensive, which is why they are so expensive. Here in Fairbanks, where oak is $4.00 per board foot, materials alone for a simple oak stair cost about $1,000. Labor might run $2,000 to $3,000. By tackling the job yourself, you can save a lot of money. In many cases, the money you save will allow you to build an elegant hardwood staircase with a nice balustrade for the price of a carpeted stairway built by a contractor.

The importance of planning. It's natural for someone who has built or remodeled his own house to follow through by completing the finish work, including the stairs. Unlike other finish work, however, stairs require detailed planning early on. A staircase isn't easy to upgrade later when more time and money are available; it's integral with its surroundings, so each step from framing to molding must be considered well ahead of time.

It often happens that, in the rush to get the framing done, the stairwell is sited as an afterthought. This invariably results in a stair with a subtle defect that ruins what could otherwise be the most pleasing part of the house. Sure, you can get used to ducking your head or shortening your stride to avoid tripping on a mis-sized riser, but it's far better to get the stair right in the first place. This applies to the details too, like the balusters, rails and skirtboards. It is of course frustrating to have to think about finish woodwork when all you want to do is get a roof over your head, but force yourself to slow down and take your time. It will be worth it.

A word of encouragement: building a stair is not a project to be taken casually, nor should it be an overwhelming, anxiety-producing ordeal. Taken step by step, stairbuilding is well within the capability of anyone with average tool skills. I hope that you'll find it a satisfying and confidence-building experience.

Acknowledgements. This book could not have been done without the synergistic help of the fine staff at The Taunton Press. In particular I would like to thank Jim Hall, who has generously given his friendship and encouragement. His good cheer is a constant inspiration. Also thanks to friend and editor Paul Bertorelli, who made the difficult process of turning words into a book enjoyable.

A model like this one, which Schuttner built for the accompanying videotape, is one way to plan a stair, but a scale drawing is more than sufficient.

Basic Stair Design

Chapter 1

Most people hate to give up space to a set of stairs. Somehow it's hard to accept the idea that floor space occupied by stairs wouldn't be better devoted to a grand kitchen or a larger living room. Even some of the architects I've worked with seem unwilling to allow enough of the floor plan for construction of a proper stairway.

Yet we all realize, if only subconsciously, that stairs have a purpose other than just getting us from one floor to the next. As our understanding of how we're affected by our surroundings grows, we realize that many parts of a house have functions beyond the most obvious. So it is with stairs.

Ascending stairs is not like walking through a door. The stairway is the only point in the house where we can gradually climb out of one room and into another, without really being entirely in one or the other. The stairway is a place to make a grand entrance or merely to sit in peace. As anyone who has ever slid down a banister will attest, a stairway is a ready-made playground, despite parents' wishes to the contrary.

It seems a shame to relegate such an important part of the house to some forgotten corner or to confinement between two walls. A stairway should be a conspicuous part of the house, placed squarely within the social happenings of the rooms it serves. In addition, the stair's basic design—its shape, method of construction and materials—should complement its location in the overall plan. There is very little point in building an expansive straight stair in a small room that would look better with an L-shaped stair.

With both the functional and psychological aspects of stair design in mind, I'll spend this chapter looking at stair siting ideas. In addition, I'll discuss the common designs for basic stairs, code requirements and construction methods. After that, I'll move right to a step-by-step explanation of how stairs are constructed.

Where to put the staircase

Well before framing starts, you should have a definite idea of where the stairs will be located. This applies to first-floor to second-floor stairs as well as to basement stairs. If you're building from plans, the stairs may be drawn in, though not necessarily in the best spot.

Almost all plans have a plan view of the stairs. A complex stair may have a plan view, plus an elevation and a section view giving specific information about landing heights, rise and run, railings and so on. If the client has requested it and is willing to pay for it, the architect may draw additional sections that give complete details on stair construction (see Figure 1 on p. 6).

It's funny, but clients sometimes think they can save money by not having the architect work out these details, figuring the carpenter will do it on site. Nothing gets built, however, until the details are worked out, so sooner or later, somebody has to do it.

No matter how detailed the plans, the stair as drawn may not conform to reality. You will often have to move the stair a bit to match existing conditions. Don't go overboard, though. The stairwell has to be integrated with halls, doors and walls, and moving one has a domino effect. The architect may have used a "stock" stairwell dimension on the plans that will yield an undesirable tread or riser dimension. Stairs are very site-specific. Small changes in the plan are the norm, so don't be afraid to make them.

Stair siting. Several things need to be considered in siting stairs. First and foremost is function: stairs should be oriented so that they're easy to find and negotiate. Stairs are often placed close to the front door so that it's obvious, upon entering the house, how to get from one floor to the next. This is sensible enough, but don't site the stair near the door if doing so will make it difficult to negotiate.

Figure 1: How Stairs are Depicted on Drawings

Some plans show simple plan views.

Others show elevations and detailed tread and riser designs.

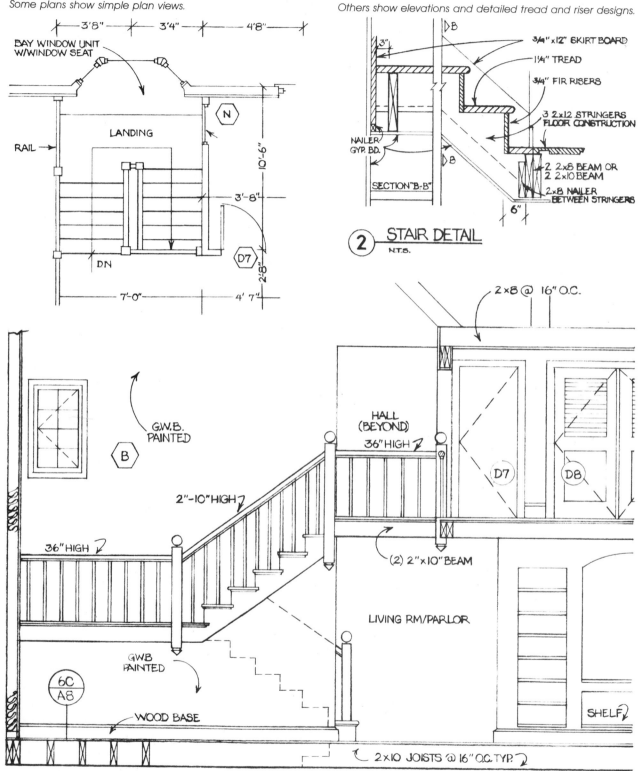

BAY WINDOW UNIT
W/WINDOW SEAT

3'8"   3'4"   4'8"

RAIL

LANDING

N

10'-6"

3'-8"

2'-8"

DN

D7

7'-0"   4'7"

3" 3/4"x12" SKIRT BOARD

1 1/4" TREAD

3/4" FIR RISERS

3 2x12 STRINGERS
FLOOR CONSTRUCTION

NAILER
GYP. BD.

B

2 2x8 BEAM OR
2 2x10 BEAM

2x8 NAILER
BETWEEN STRINGERS

SECTION "B-B"

6"

2 — STAIR DETAIL
N.T.S.

2x8 @ 16" O.C.

G.W.B.
PAINTED

B

HALL
(BEYOND)
36" HIGH

D7

D8

2"-10" HIGH

36" HIGH

(2) 2"x10" BEAM

LIVING RM/PARLOR

GWB
PAINTED

6C
A8

WOOD BASE

SHELF

2x10 JOISTS @ 16" O.C. TYP.

One book I've found helpful in siting stairs is Christopher Alexander's *A Pattern Language*. Alexander and his co-authors argue rightly that stairs are sometimes seen solely as an architectural means of making a statement about the house. As such, they are placed so people can see them. This sometimes means plopping the stairs right next to a seldom used front door. That's fine for the house guests visiting for the first time but not so good for those using the stair every day.

Try to locate stairs so they are readily accessible from the common areas of the house as well as visible from the entrance. This helps integrate the stair into the room, functionally and socially. Common areas include entryways, foyers, halls, living rooms, dining rooms and kitchens. It won't be possible to access all these areas equally, but compromise to serve as many of them as possible (see Figure 2).

Unless I intend to divide a room into two separate areas, I try to avoid placing stairs in the middle of the room or between two walls. Stairs open on one side become a part of the room. Stairs should be placed so traffic flows naturally. It doesn't make sense to march across a large room every time you want to go upstairs. A centrally located stair will be more obvious from the ground floor, and it will serve as a hub to reach the upstairs rooms. A centrally located stair has a social function too. It represents extra seating for casual visitors, keeping them in touch but not in the way.

The stair exit at the upper level is sometimes compromised by the stair's location on the main floor. It may, for example, be too close to a bedroom door or have to turn a sharp corner into a hall. The upstairs exit is usually purely functional, whereas the downstairs site has to take into account the way the stair will look.

Don't forget either that a stairway occupies a three-dimensional volume. That means its height can produce an unpleasant, cavernous feeling. Adding a landing or a window will help. So will hanging a painting or tapestry on a stairwell wall, which is, after all, likely to be the only two-story wall in the house.

Because the area under the main stair is narrow and oddly shaped, it is difficult to put to use. Not surprisingly, that space is ideal as the stairwell and ceiling for another staircase. That's why basement stairs are often located right under the main staircase. This is such a logical design that someone who is unfamiliar with the house will typically know where to find the basement stairs without being told.

Figure 2: Siting Stairs

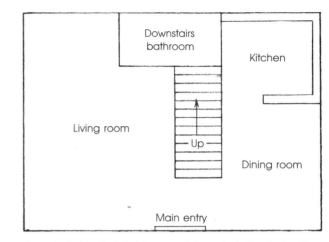

A centrally located stair is accessible and obvious but splits the floor plan. Space underneath can be used for closets or a small bath.

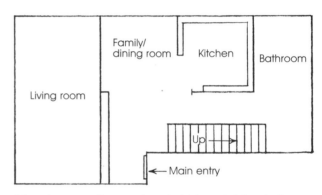

A long house easily accepts a straight-run stair located near the main entry. But in a square floor plan, a straight-run stair uses lots of floor space.

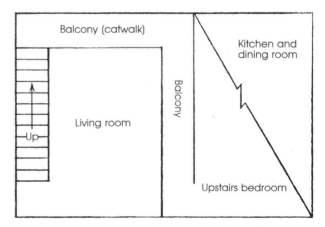

A stair located in one corner is dramatic but requires a hike across the house to get upstairs.

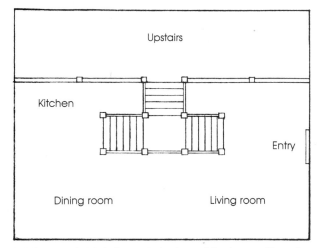

This T-shaped stair is the main feature of the house. It's well located functionally, aesthetically and socially but consumes lots of floor space.

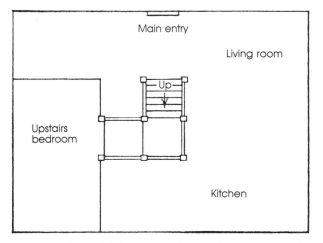

A central L-shaped stair is accessible from the main entry. It divides the house, yet still provides an open feeling.

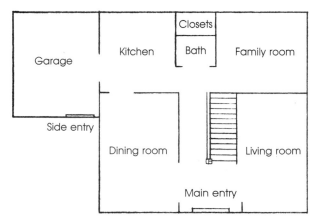

A common plan for older homes, this centrally located straight case gives good access from the main entry, but the most used entry is through the garage.

Stair types

There are literally dozens of stair types, but I'll look at just three here: the straight stair, the L-shaped stair and the open-riser ladder. Each is well-suited to a particular application, and taken together, one of these types (or a variation) will meet virtually any stair design requirement (see Figure 3).

The straight stair. This is the simplest stair design. It consists of two or three carriages or stringers supporting a series of treads and risers. As I'll explain a bit later, the straight stair can be a very simple affair, say a basement utility stair that doesn't even have risers, or a very complex structure that requires a lot of fussy joinery.

In general, straight stairs are easy to construct but often difficult to find room for on the floor plan. They're long and skinny, so in a house with conventional 8-ft. ceilings a straight case will be at least 10 ft. long. Add to that landings at both ends, and you can see that a straight staircase takes up a lot of space. A straight stair usually fits best against one wall, and because of its long span, the stair may need framing underneath to keep it from feeling bouncy.

To add interest to what is otherwise a visually boring design, you can put a landing halfway down a straight run of stairs. Although this does introduce some variety, it also eats up additional floor space. A straight case that ascends predictably between two walls can be improved visually by removing one of the walls so the stair is open on one side. This, of course, will require a rail system.

The L-shaped stair. This design is versatile because it can be tucked into a corner without looking cramped. For the equivalent rise, an L-shaped stairway actually needs a little more floor space than a straight stair. But you don't have to find one long, straight chunk of floor space, which is difficult in a small house. An L-shaped stair, also called a quarter-turn, is more appealing because your eye won't be bored by a vast expanse of regularly spaced treads and risers. Some people say an L-shaped stair is safer than a straight case because the landing provides a place to rest, and in the event of a slip, you won't have as far to fall. It's possible to turn an L-shape into a T by building two flights of stairs from a common landing. Although this would no longer fit into a corner and could hardly be considered space-saving, it is useful if you are trying to divide a room and want to maintain symmetry.

Variations of the L-shape include the switchback and the U-shape or double-L, also shown in Figure 3. These are also called half-turn stairs. The switchback makes a 180° turn at one large landing or at two smaller landings divided by a drop of one step. This stair is very compact, requiring floor space of only about 6 ft. by 8 ft. The switchback is a good choice when there's a lot of rise but not much floor space.

Figure 3: Stair Types

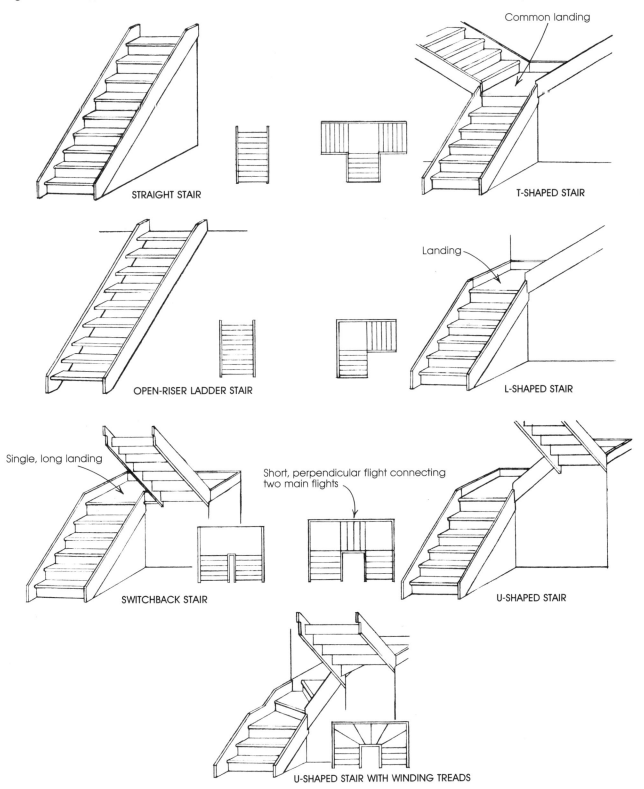

Common landing

STRAIGHT STAIR

T-SHAPED STAIR

OPEN-RISER LADDER STAIR

Landing

L-SHAPED STAIR

Single, long landing

SWITCHBACK STAIR

Short, perpendicular flight connecting two main flights

U-SHAPED STAIR

U-SHAPED STAIR WITH WINDING TREADS

Figure 4: Stair Nomenclature

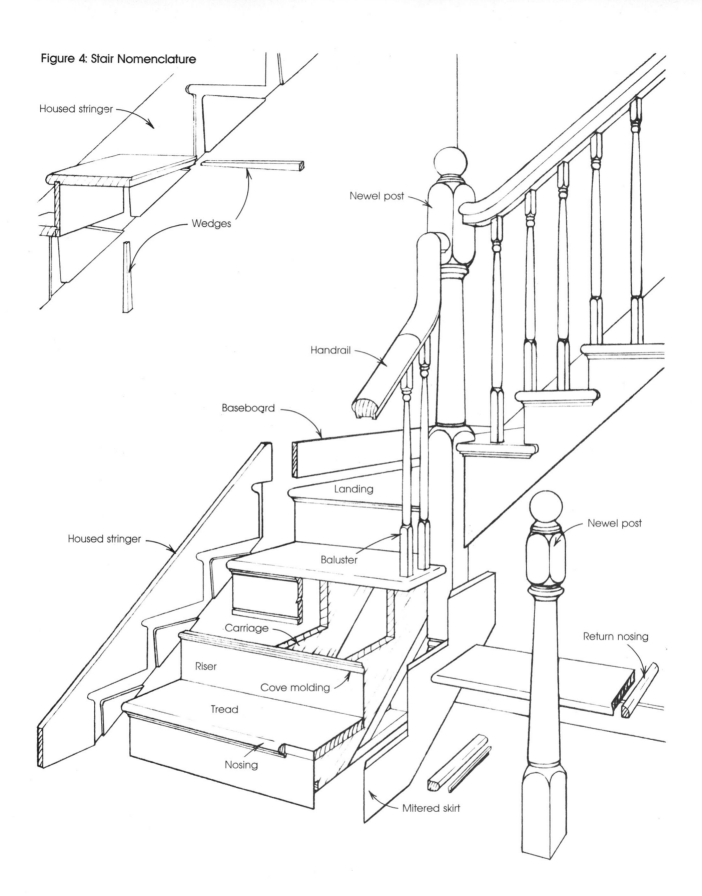

Housed stringer

Wedges

Newel post

Handrail

Baseboard

Landing

Housed stringer

Baluster

Carriage

Riser

Cove molding

Tread

Nosing

Newel post

Return nosing

Mitered skirt

The U-shape is really just a switchback in which the landing has been separated by a short straight flight. This type does use more room, but it's very dramatic. Both the switchback and the U-shape can be made even more compact by turning the corners with tight winder steps. Winders are wedge-shaped treads that split the space normally taken by the landings in half on the diagonal. From a safety point of view, winders aren't the greatest. As you can see in Figure 3 on p. 9, the treads drop about 30 in. as they swing around the central axis. This means that a slip could drop you quite a distance. Because they aren't as safe and are hard to build, I use winders only when there's not enough space to accommodate a landing.

The open-riser ladder. The ladder stair, shown in Figure 3 on p. 9, is a good utility stair when it's made of common framing lumber. It can also be made of hardwood, if you want to dress it up. Built with a shallow rise, the ladder can be negotiated conventionally; with a very steep rise, the absence of risers makes ascending it more like climbing a ladder. The steep ladder stair works well when floor space is acutely limited.

For the sake of comparison, using nominal 3-ft. wide treads, a straight-run stair without a mid-flight landing will use just under 35 sq. ft. of floor space. An L-shaped stair adds a landing and requires about 40 sq. ft. A U-shaped or switchback stair adds two landings and needs about 50 sq. ft. A ladder type may need only 10 to 15 sq. ft. of floor space.

Construction methods

As in carpentry in general, there's no one right way to build a staircase. Even a relatively simple straight stair can be constructed in any of several ways. The nice thing about building your own stair is that you can pick the method that suits your aesthetic goals, your budget and the tools and skills you happen to have. In this section, I'll describe some common stair-construction methods, and later I'll show how these methods relate to specific stair designs.

But first, some definitions. Stairbuilding has its own vocabulary, and understanding it is an important part of learning to build stairs. Things can get confusing, though, because terms are used inconsistently from one part of the country to another. What one carpenter calls a carriage, for example, another calls a stringer, and everyone is occasionally puzzled by the difference between a baluster and a balustrade. Stair nomenclature is shown in Figure 4.

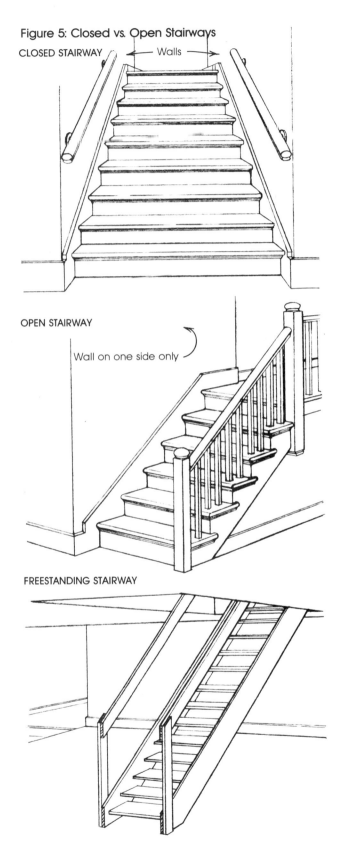

Figure 5: Closed vs. Open Stairways

CLOSED STAIRWAY ← Walls →

OPEN STAIRWAY

Wall on one side only

FREESTANDING STAIRWAY

The word "stairway" is a catchall term often used to describe either the stairs themselves or the general area where the stairs are located. I like to think of the stairway as occupying a three-dimensional volume called the **stairwell.** The opening in the upper level through which the stair ascends is called the **stairwell opening.** The completed stairway (that is, the steps, rails, landings, trim and so on) is correctly called a **staircase.** If a stair has walls on both sides it is called a **closed stair.** If it has one or both sides without walls it is an **open stair.** Open and closed stairs are shown in Figure 5 on p. 11.

In its less grand form, the staircase is sometimes called simply a set of steps. Each step is composed of one vertical part, called a **riser,** and one horizontal part, called a **tread.** This kind of construction is called a **closed-riser stair.** Sometimes, however, as in the open-riser ladder stair, there are no risers: the steps consist simply of treads let into diagonal supporting members. In either case, the diagonal members that support the treads are called **carriages** or **stringers.** Their job is to provide structural support for the treads as they climb up to the next level.

Tread design. In very simple stairs, the treads rest on 1x4 cleats nailed to the carriages. This construction requires the least effort but yields poor durability because the cleats continually work loose. Glue and screws or steel angle irons in place of the 1x4s help, but I don't use this method except for temporary stairs. A more permanent variation is to cut dadoes into the carriages into which the treads are inserted, as shown in Figure 6. If the stair needs to look a little more polished, make a stopped dado instead. This construction method, which I call dadoed, is discussed more fully in Chapter 6.

By far the most common construction method is the **cut carriage.** In this method, the carriage is notched

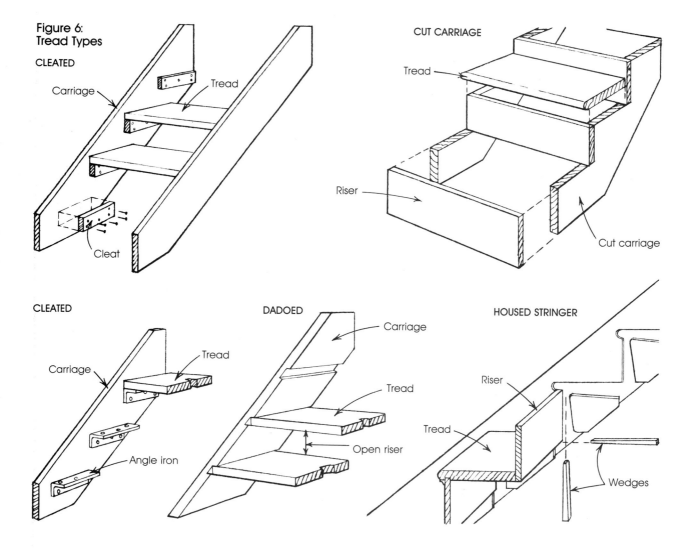

Figure 6:
Tread Types

CLEATED

Carriage

Tread

Cleat

CUT CARRIAGE

Tread

Riser

Cut carriage

CLEATED

Carriage

Tread

Angle iron

DADOED

Carriage

Tread

Open riser

HOUSED STRINGER

Riser

Tread

Wedges

sawtooth fashion to support treads and risers. The carriages are usually made of rough framing lumber that will be covered with some kind of trim later on. Sometimes, as in a basement stair, the rough carriages will be exposed, in which case the risers are often left off. This is an **open-riser stair.** In some contemporary architecture, the carriages are made of a nice hardwood like oak or ash and are deliberately exposed.

In **open stairs,** that is, where one side butts to a wall, the wall-side treads are sometimes supported by letting them into mortises cut into a wide, decorative piece called a **housed stringer,** or **closed skirt.** The mortises, which are slightly tapered, exactly follow the zigzag outline of the carriages, which support the treads on the open side of the stair. Wedges glued into the tapers hold the treads tightly in the mortises. This Is a very good sys-

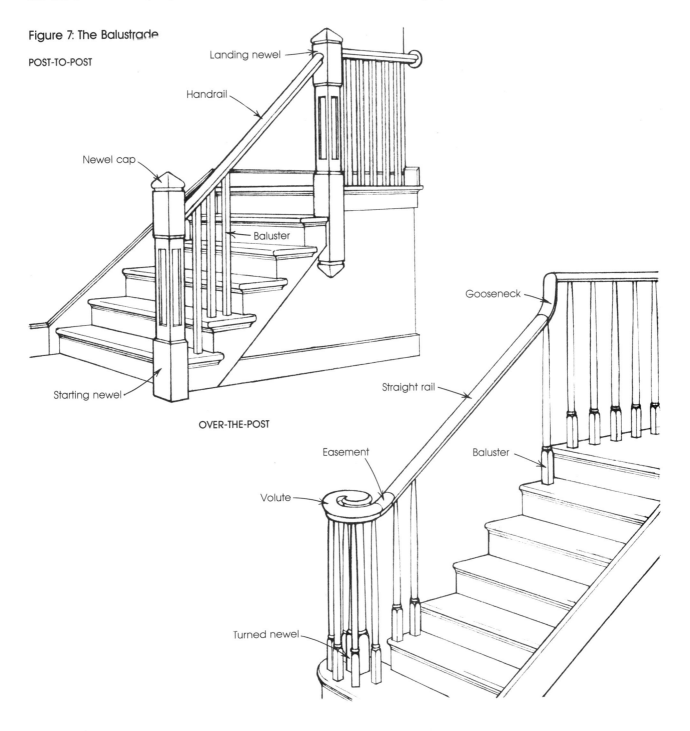

Figure 7: The Balustrade

POST-TO-POST

Landing newel

Handrail

Newel cap

Baluster

Starting newel

OVER-THE-POST

Gooseneck

Straight rail

Baluster

Easement

Volute

Turned newel

tem, and is the way stairs were traditionally built. It's very labor intensive, though, and requires a lot of patient work with the router to achieve a good fit. More on this later.

A note on terminology: In the videotape, you will hear me call housed stringers "skirtboards," but this isn't precisely correct. A **skirtboard** is really just a piece of trim meant to cover the structural carriages—it has no structural function of its own. The terms **carriage** and **stringer** are used interchangeably in some parts of the country. When applied to a skirtboard, the term **open** means that the board has been cut to follow the sawtooth pattern of the carriage so that the treads and risers lap over it. **Closed** means that the skirtboard has no sawtooth cuts, so the treads and risers butt right to it, rather than lapping over it.

It's not unusual for housed stringers to be used in combination with cut carriages (as in the L-shaped stairway that I built for this book). The housed stringer against the wall is a structural member that actually supports the treads. The skirtboard on the opposite end of the treads—an open skirtboard because it follows the sawtooth pattern—is decorative, with the structural support being provided by a cut carriage behind the skirtboard. Because the risers miter into the skirt, it's also referred to as a **mitered skirt.** One can also eliminate the housed stringer and just butt the treads and risers into a skirtboard. As with the mitered skirt, however, this requires a cut carriage underneath to support the treads.

Handrails. All of this leads logically to handrails and balustrades. The **balustrade** is the entire handrail assembly, including newel posts, the individual balusters and the handrailing itself. The word balustrade calls to mind a grand flowing handrail ending in an elaborately carved volute, but an elegant balustrade really doesn't have to be fancy. **Balusters** are the small vertical members, usually two per step, that support the handrail as it climbs the stair. **Newels** are the large vertical posts where the hand-

Figure 8: Stair Code Requirements

Minimum width must be between finished drywall surfaces.

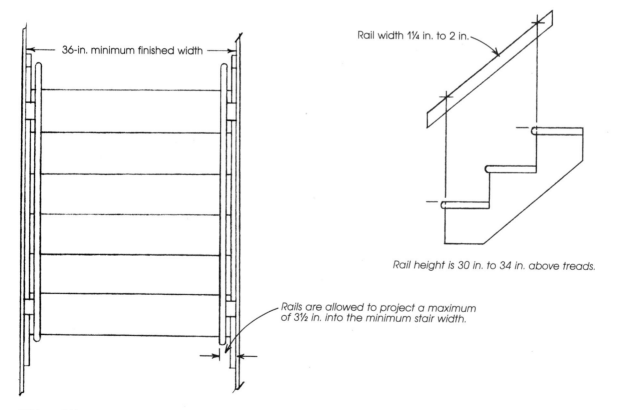

36-in. minimum finished width

Rail width 1¼ in. to 2 in.

Rail height is 30 in. to 34 in. above treads.

Rails are allowed to project a maximum of 3½ in. into the minimum stair width.

Skirts and trim can project into the minimum width 1½ in. on each side.

rails terminate. There's usually a **starting newel** at the base of the stairs and a **landing newel, or angle newel,** at each landing. On very long spans, there may be intermediate newels as well. The **handrail,** the part you actually hold onto, caps the balustrade or, if there is no balustrade, is simply fastened to the wall. Figure 7 on p. 13 shows the two major kinds of handrail systems, **post-to-post** and **over-the-post.**

Stair design and the code

Many factors need to be considered in designing stairs, with overall size leading the list. Often, the most visually appealing or comfortable size just won't work. To complicate matters, building codes require minimum sizes, so what you end up with may represent a compromise between what you want and what the code says you have to have. It's okay to exceed code standards, but don't ignore them. Codes vary quite a bit, and as I don't have the space to explain all of them, I'll give general advice. Check with your local building inspector for specifics.

A stair needs to be wide enough to allow two people to pass when they meet. Most codes give 36 in. as the minimum width from finished wall to finished wall. Some codes allow 30-in. widths for "private" stairs that serve one room or for basement steps. Since the width must be between finished walls, your rough framing will have to allow for drywall or plaster. However, skirtboards and trim may project into the minimum width up to 1½ in. on each side. I find 36 in. to be barely adequate, so I usually aim for 40 in. to 42 in. between finished walls. Keep in mind that skirtboards will decrease the overall width and that factory-made treads are sold in standard lengths. An extra ½ in. in width could mean $100 extra for longer treads. The code usually requires that stairs wider than 44 in. have handrails on both sides. Figure 8 shows various dimensions required by code.

Figure 9: Rise and Run

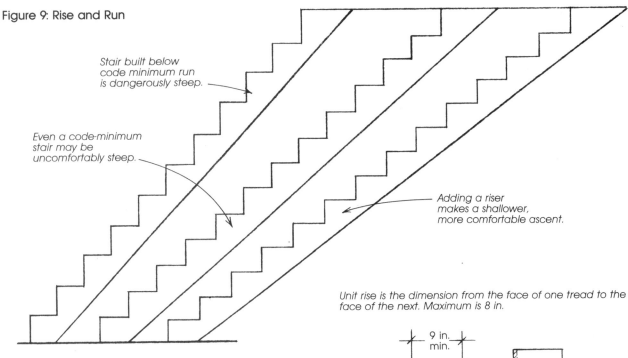

Stair built below code minimum run is dangerously steep.

Even a code-minimum stair may be uncomfortably steep.

Adding a riser makes a shallower, more comfortable ascent.

Unit rise is the dimension from the face of one tread to the face of the next. Maximum is 8 in.

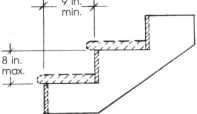

9 in. min.

8 in. max.

Unit run is the dimension from the face of one riser to the face of the next. Minimum is 9 in.

Rise and run. Rise and run get a lot of attention when stair designs are worked out, and rightly so. These two elements affect almost every aspect of the stair. Total rise is the vertical distance the stair must negotiate, from finished floor on the lower level to finished floor on the upper level. Total run is the horizontal distance the stair covers, from the beginning of the first tread to the end of the last tread.

I'll get into the specifics of calculating rise and run later, but for now suffice it to say that you can estimate rise from the plans, then measure it exactly once the framing and decking are done. The total rise is divided up to give us the rise of each step. This rise is exactly the same for every step and is referred to as the unit rise (see Figure 9 on p. 15). To allow for joinery, the riser itself is a bit wider than the unit rise.

The total run can't really be measured on site but is arrived at by adding up all the unit runs—the width of each tread from the face of one riser to the face of the next riser. Keep in mind that unit run isn't the total width of the tread, however, because each tread has a rounded nosing that extends beyond the face of the riser. This is illustrated in Figure 9.

There are guidelines for rise and run. Codes generally say that maximum unit rise for a main residential stairway shouldn't exceed 8 in. and unit run shouldn't be less than 9 in. Using these two numbers, we'll get a stair at the maximum steepness allowed by the code. However, these minimum conditions don't give us a particularly comfortable staircase, just one that's not dangerously steep. It's the worst-case scenario. Reducing the unit rise or increasing the unit run will reduce the stair's angle of ascent. Commercial applications allow 4 in. to 7 in. for rise and a minimum of 11 in. of run.

The idea is to choose a combination of rise and run that will produce a comfortable stair while still allowing it to ascend in the floor space allotted to it. As is often the case, there's a rule-of-thumb formula for this:

Unit rise + unit run = 17 in. to 18 in.

There are a couple of other versions of the formula:

Twice the unit rise + unit run = 24 in. to 25 in.
    and
Unit rise × unit run = 70 in. to 75 in.

I think the first formula is the easiest to remember, but you can take your pick. If we plug the code standards into our formula, that is, 8 in. of rise plus 9 in. of run, the result is 17 in. I don't like to exceed 7 in. of unit rise, however, because I feel it creates an uncomfortable, hurried step. If space is tight, I'll use as much as 7½ in. of rise, but when I don't have to worry about space I prefer 6½ in. Some may feel that this is too little rise, meaning

that it takes too long to climb the stairs. But I disagree. The lower rise imparts a nice feel to the stairway, and there's less chance of a slip.

For planning purposes, I try to figure the rough rise and run of the staircase even as I'm framing the house. That way, I can size the stairwell opening accordingly and allow enough floor space for the stair. Typically, in a house with 8-ft. walls and 2x10 floor joists, I know that I'll have 14 risers. If I divide the total rise by 14, I'll arrive at unit rise, which is a little over 7½ in. (In the videotape, I actually used 7¹¹⁄₁₆ in.) If I want a smaller unit rise, I'll divide by 15. By adding that extra rise I have of course added one more tread and made the staircase that much longer.

By plugging my unit rise into one of the formulas, I can calculate unit run. Adding up all the unit runs will give me the total run and an idea of how much horizontal space the staircase will take up. At this point, I'm doing a juggling act. If lowering my unit rise to a dimension I like adds an extra tread, I might not have enough room. I could then shorten the unit run a little to compress the staircase horizontally, so long as I stay within my formula. Of course, altering rise and run also affects headroom, so I may have to change my stairwell opening size. You can see why planning ahead pays off.

Beware of squeezing the unit run too hard, especially on a stair with wooden treads. The treads are slippery, and once you get under 10 in. of run, you'll find that falls become a problem. You can get by with steeper stairs or shorter unit runs on carpeted stairs, because the carpet provides better traction.

Headroom. The distance measured vertically from the top of any tread to anything that you might hit your head on is called headroom. It's probably the most abused specification in stair design. It's possible to have an otherwise perfectly designed stairway go through a hole in the floor that's simply too small. There's always something on the upper floor, such as a closet, bathroom or hallway, that desperately needs the space being taken up by the stairwell opening.

Codes generally say a stair should have a minimum of 6 ft. 8 in. of headroom. As a person who is 6 ft. 6 in. tall, I can tell you that this isn't enough. The fear of banging my head makes me slump as I go up and down the stair. I recommend that you try for a minimum of 7 ft. of headroom. The most obvious way to increase headroom is to make the stairwell opening larger. If headroom problems occur only where there are floor joists, I try to angle the ends of my cut joists or maybe just frame the stairwell opening larger and let the plywood cantilever out to catch any partition framing above (see Figure 10). Another way to solve headroom problems is to make the stairway steeper by altering the rise and run. This sometimes creates more problems than it solves, but it can be a solution in a tight spot.

Depending on the building code, a stair with a total rise of more than 12 ft. must have a landing at mid-flight. The landing has to be at least the width of the stair and as long as the stairway is wide. In other words, the minimum condition is a square landing whose sides are equal to the stair width. It's okay to make the landing longer than the stair's width.

If a door at the top of the stair opens toward the stair, you'll need a landing that's at least as long as the door is wide. This provides a safe stopping point for opening and closing the door. Even if the door opens away from the stair, it's a good idea to provide a small landing to allow a person to find a light switch before descending the steps. When space permits, follow these landing requirements at the bottom of the stair too.

Handrails and balustrades. Building codes generally require handrails on any stair that has three or more risers, regardless of width. An open stair that's less than 44 in. wide with a wall on one side can get by with one rail,

providing it's on the open side. Stairs wider than 44 in. or stairs with no adjacent walls have to have rails on both sides. Closed stairs need railings on both sides if they are more than 44 in. wide.

According to most building codes, rails are supposed to be between 30 in. and 34 in. above the leading edge of a tread, as shown in Figure 8 on p. 14. Rails are allowed to project 3½ in. from each wall into the minimum stair width. In other words, you don't have to take the rail projection into account when you figure the minimum width. Individual balusters on both handrails and the guardrails that surround landings should be no greater than 6 in. apart, edge to edge, but I prefer to space them closer, say about 4 in.

There should be no less than 1½ in. between the wall and the rail for your hands to slide. The cross section of the rail should be between 1¼ in. and 2 in. wide. These are good reference numbers for designing your own railings. Or, if you prefer, lumberyard rail hardware will meet these specifications.

Figure 10: Headroom Solutions

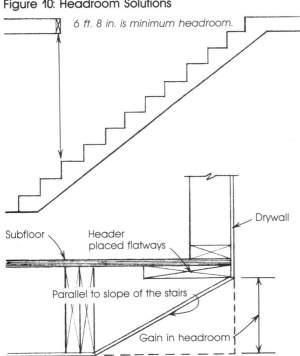

6 ft. 8 in. is minimum headroom.

Drywall

Subfloor Header placed flatways

Parallel to slope of the stairs

Gain in headroom

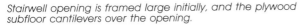

Stairwell opening is framed large initially, and the plywood subfloor cantilevers over the opening.

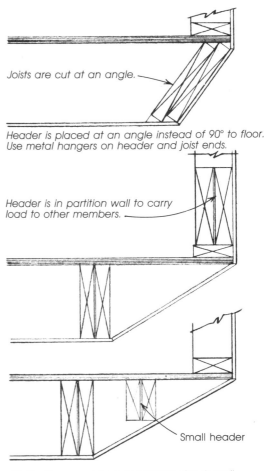

Joists are cut at an angle.

Header is placed at an angle instead of 90° to floor. Use metal hangers on header and joist ends.

Header is in partition wall to carry load to other members.

Small header

All situations require small blocking for drywall.

Materials and structure

In this book and videotape, I show how to build both carpeted stairs and traditional hardwood stairs made of oak. For a carpeted stair or utility stairs, I use 2x12 lumber for the carriages. Normally, I use three carriages, both because codes recommend them for stairs wider than 30 in. and because the middle carriage reduces bounce. This is true even for the L-shaped stair, whose carriages have a much shorter free span. A third carriage is vital on open-riser stairs because there are no risers to provide additional structural support.

On very long spans, say up to 14 ft., even three carriages won't prevent bouncing. Some kind of supportive framing will be needed. In a staircase that's closed on one or both sides, I nail carriages to the wall framing for additional support. It's also possible to double the carriage on the open side of a stairway if additional framing underneath is objectionable.

On carpeted stairs, I use 1⅛-in. plywood for the treads and ¾-in. plywood for the risers. I try to buy underlayment-grade plywood because it's supposed to have fewer voids and is sanded smooth on one side, unlike CDX plywood. AC-grade is fine too, but more expensive. I don't use plywood treads for other than a carpeted stair because the face lamination will chip or wear, and plywood edges are not attractive. Trim for a carpeted stair, the skirtboard mainly, can be painted pine or fir or varnished hardwood.

Hardwood stairs, whose treads and risers are intended to be seen, are usually made of red or white oak. Standard treads are $1\frac{1}{16}$ in. thick and can be bought factory-made in various lengths and widths, with a rounded nosing molded into one edge. All you have to do is cut them to the exact length and width you want. Factory treads are usually laminated from three to five flatsawn strips glued together. The laminated construction reduces warping and cupping. You could glue up your own treads, but it's cheaper and faster to buy them.

Risers are another story. They're typically $\frac{3}{4}$ in. thick and up to 8 in. wide. I prefer to make my own out of solid boards instead of buying factory-laminated parts because all those glue joints on both the treads and the risers make the stair look like a zebra. In place of oak you can of course substitute various hardwoods, including cherry, walnut, maple, ash or even a hard-wearing softwood like vertical-grain fir or yellow pine. If the treads and risers are to be painted instead of finished clear, use pine or fir.

The housed stringer on an oak staircase is a structural element and as such needs to be thicker than $\frac{3}{4}$-in. stock. I use 1-in. to $1\frac{1}{2}$-in. thick lumber. This extra thickness is also necessary to allow for $\frac{1}{2}$-in. deep mortises. The board is at least $9\frac{1}{2}$ in. wide and is of the same type of wood as the treads and risers. Because the housed stringer is attached and therefore supported by the wall framing, it is unnecessary to use a greater thickness.

The mitered skirt on the open side is not a structural element and need only be $\frac{3}{4}$ in. thick. It could be thinner, but this thickness makes it easy to mate with the risers, which are also $\frac{3}{4}$ in. thick. This application requires a little wider board, usually about 11 in.

In ideal circumstances, the stair's overall size will determine how large the stairwell will be. In remodel work, however, the stair will have to fit the space available.

The Stairwell

Chapter 2

Perhaps because it gets covered with drywall and trim, the stairwell opening doesn't account for much during the early phases of house building. I think some carpenters view the stairwell opening as nothing but a bothersome interuption in the quick rhythm of hanging floor joists. But just as a square and level foundation leads to accurate framing, so too does a properly designed stairwell result in a safe, comfortable stair.

As I explained in Chapter 1, the stairwell opening is a framed hole in the floor through which the stair emerges onto the next level. In addition, it provides a solid anchor for the tops of the carriages and, sometimes, support for walls on the second floor. The framing of the stairwell opening should be planned right from the beginning because its size and shape will sharply limit how much you can manipulate rise and run to arrive at a comfortable stair. The stairwell opening is not something you want to have to come back to later by cutting out a few joists and inserting others.

You'll be confronted with two situations when building the stairwell, one ideal and one makeshift. The ideal situation is to be able to locate the stair exactly where you want it, pick the rise and run and then size the opening accordingly. In makeshift circumstances, you'll have to settle for a stair that fits the floor plan, then do your best on rise and run and arrange the framing to suit the stairwell opening.

Sizing the opening

Let's consider the ideal situation first, one in which the stair can be located just where you would like it. To size the opening, you'll first choose a comfortable unit rise and unit run, then go on to calculate total run. Typically, the total rise in a two-story house (finished floor to finished floor) is about 107½ in., which is what I use in the videotape. This assumes standard studs with double top plates, ¾-in. plywood decking on the second floor and 2x10 floor joists.

Having estimated 107½ in. as our total rise, we need to divide that by whatever we consider to be a desirable unit rise. This will yield the number of risers. Choosing a 7-in. rise as a starting place results in 15.35 risers. Obviously the number of risers has to be even, so round off to the nearest whole number, 15 in this case. Dividing 15 into 107½ in. gives a unit rise of 7.16 in., or about 7⁵⁄₃₂ in. This is a little higher than the initial choice, but it's still an acceptable rise.

Since the total number of treads is always one less than the total number of risers, this stair will have 14 treads. To find unit run, plug the rise into the formula explained on p. 16 (which yields 10 in. in this case), then multiply the total number of treads by the unit run to arrive at total run. Total run in this case is 140 in.

My rule of thumb is that the length of the stairwell opening should be at least equal to the total run. In a house with 8-ft. ceilings, this will result in a headroom of about 7 ft. 6 in. If the headroom isn't enough for you, you'll have to make some adjustments, as described below. One other thing to consider when calculating stairwell length is how the carriages will be fastened. In the example I've just explained, the header that forms the stairwell opening is actually the top riser, as shown in the top and middle drawings in Figure 12 on p. 23. The carriages are nailed to the framing via a plywood hangerboard or attached with a metal strap. In these instances, total run is figured to the stair-side of the floor framing.

An alternative design is shown in the bottom drawing in Figure 12. Here, the top tread of the carriage is actually aligned with the framing on the second level. The advantage of this is that the carriage's greatest bearing surface rests directly against the floor framing, and the plywood subfloor ties the stair firmly to the framing.

Figure 11: Stairwell Opening

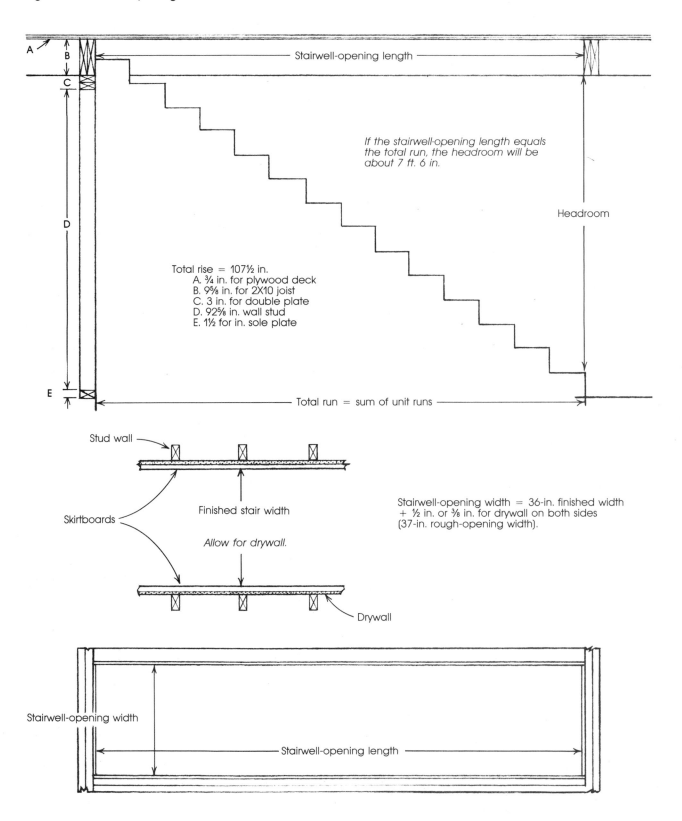

Stairwell-opening length

If the stairwell-opening length equals the total run, the headroom will be about 7 ft. 6 in.

Headroom

Total rise = 107½ in.
  A. ¾ in. for plywood deck
  B. 9⅝ in. for 2X10 joist
  C. 3 in. for double plate
  D. 92⅝ in. wall stud
  E. 1½ for in. sole plate

Total run = sum of unit runs

Stud wall

Skirtboards

Finished stair width

Allow for drywall.

Drywall

Stairwell-opening width = 36-in. finished width + ½ in. or ⅜ in. for drywall on both sides (37-in. rough-opening width).

Stairwell-opening width

Stairwell-opening length

Of course, there's a subtle trap here. You must remember to figure total run to the face of the top riser, not to the stairwell framing. Then add one unit run to the total run to arrive at the stairwell length. If you don't remember to do this, the carriages will fit into the opening, but headroom will be compromised. The top tread is actually formed by cantilevering the floor sheathing into the stairwell opening.

Headroom is a simple concept to deal with if you keep a few things in mind. If the stairwell length isn't smaller than the total run of the stair, headroom will not be a problem in a house with standard or taller ceiling heights. Here the headroom is simply the ceiling height minus the height of the first unit rise. If the opening is shorter than the total run, each unit run it is shorter will decrease the headroom by an additional unit rise. An opening may be only a partial unit run smaller; technically, this would amount to the same fraction of the unit rise decrease in headroom, but I prefer to subtract the entire unit rise to be on the safe side. The fractional allowance could become important when things are squeezed to the minimum and codes must be met.

For the mathematically inclined, there is a formula for calculating stairwell opening size. It's shown in Figure 13 on p. 24. I find it just as easy to make a sketch to scale if I have any doubts, particularly if landings are involved. Landings in straight stairs will usually be necessary only to meet code requirements. To calculate opening requirements when landings are involved, treat the stair as two separate flights, then add the length of the landing to the total run. Headroom can then be figured with a drawing or with the formula.

Figuring stairwell-opening width is fairly easy. The opening's width should be equal to the desired finished-stair width, plus an allowance for drywall, skirtboards, paneling and so on. As explained in Chapter 1, wall-mounted railings and skirtboards are allowed by code to project into the stair's minimum width.

Dealing with tight quarters. Let's assume we have a stair whose total rise is 107½ in. that has to fit into a stairwell opening only 120 in. long. Choosing the same 7.16-in. unit rise and 10-in. unit run, we'll have a total run of about 140 in., 20 in. longer than the opening. This means that the stairwell's overhanging framing will be even with the face of the third riser. A quick sketch or the formula shows that this results in an inadequate headroom of 6 ft. 4 in.

If the headroom is too small, you have four choices: (a) eliminate one tread by increasing unit rise, (b) make the unit run shorter, (c) make the stairwell opening larger or (d) live with inadequate headroom. In this case, shortening the unit run will violate the rise and run rules, and we are assuming that structural considerations prevent us

Figure 12: Carriage-Fastening Methods

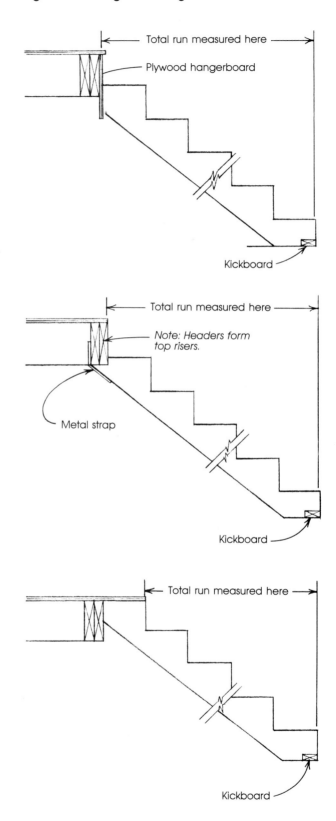

Total run measured here
Plywood hangerboard
Kickboard

Total run measured here
Note: Headers form top risers.
Metal strap
Kickboard

Total run measured here
Kickboard

from enlarging the opening. So let's increase the unit rise. This means choosing 14 risers instead of 15 to give us a unit rise of 7.65 in. or about 7¹¹⁄₁₆ in. That's a bit high, but still tolerable. There will be 13 treads instead of 14, and the total run (if we retain 10 in. as the unit run) is now 130 in. This adds 7½ in. to the headroom for a total of about 7 ft.

An L-shaped opening. The opening for an L-shaped stair is more complicated than for the straight-run stair, as the width of the stair also figures into the length of the well. One situation is where there are walls on both sides of the upper and lower flights, which means that the opening is L-shaped too. This is a little simpler in that there's no balustrade to build. Where there's a spacious floor plan on both the upper and lower floors, an L-shaped stair can ascend through a square or rectangular stairwell opening. This is a very dramatic design that gives a sense of great space.

To calculate the size of an L-shaped opening, begin with the landing. First, choose the height of the landing, which will, in effect, be just like a tread, only longer. The landing can represent any tread in the stair, though, to make things easier, the middle tread is best, as both upper and lower flights will have equal total run and total rise. Knowing the upper flight run, use Figure 14 to calculate the length and width of the stairwell opening.

There's quite a bit more detail about this in Chapter 4, which tells how to determine the landing's dimensions using the balustrade centerline as a reference point. This centerline business is fairly important because in cases where the lower stair is open and the upper stair closed, it will help you avoid having the balustrade march right into the underside of the ceiling. Also, the centerline is indispensable in getting the balustrade parts to align. If you are in doubt about the size of the opening, make it a bit larger than your estimate so you'll have room for the balustrade to pass.

Figure 13: Stairwell Length/Headroom Formula

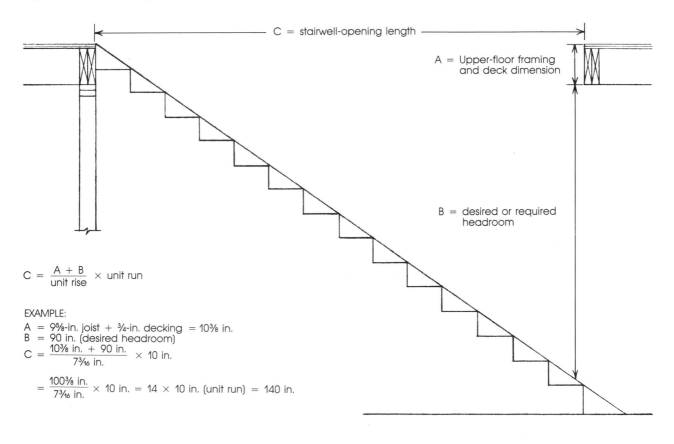

$$C = \frac{A + B}{\text{unit rise}} \times \text{unit run}$$

EXAMPLE:
A = 9⅝-in. joist + ¾-in. decking = 10⅜ in.
B = 90 in. (desired headroom)

$$C = \frac{10⅜ \text{ in.} + 90 \text{ in.}}{7³⁄₁₆ \text{ in.}} \times 10 \text{ in.}$$

$$= \frac{100⅜ \text{ in.}}{7³⁄₁₆ \text{ in.}} \times 10 \text{ in.} = 14 \times 10 \text{ in. (unit run)} = 140 \text{ in.}$$

If floor plan can't accomodate this size stairwell, plug in a smaller headroom value or a different unit rise or run.

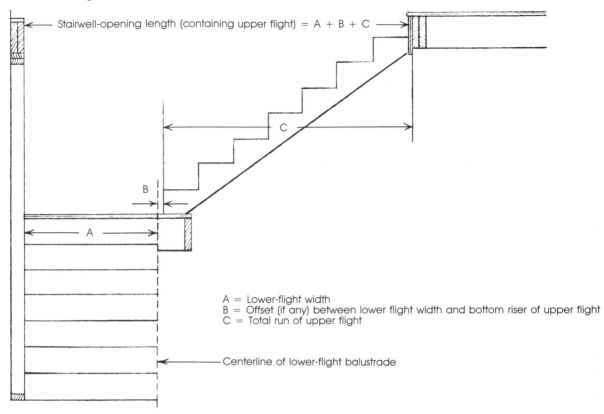

A = Lower-flight width
B = Offset (if any) between lower flight width and bottom riser of upper flight
C = Total run of upper flight

STAIRWELL LENGTH

Stairwell-opening length (containing upper flight)
= A + B + C

A = Lower-flight width
B = Offset (if any) between lower-flight width and bottom riser of upper flight
C = Total run of upper flight

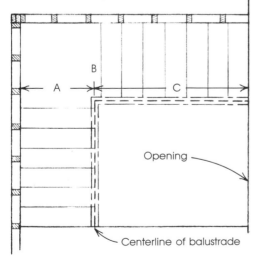

STAIRWELL WIDTH

Stairwell-opening width (containing lower flight)
= A + B + C

A = Upper-flight width
B = Offset (if any) between upper-flight width and face of top riser in lower flight
C = Total run of lower flight

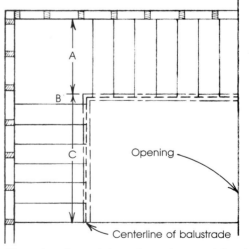

Dimensions for an L-shaped opening are determined according to Figure 15, and stud walls are built before the stair is installed.

Figure 15: Stairwell Framing Plan

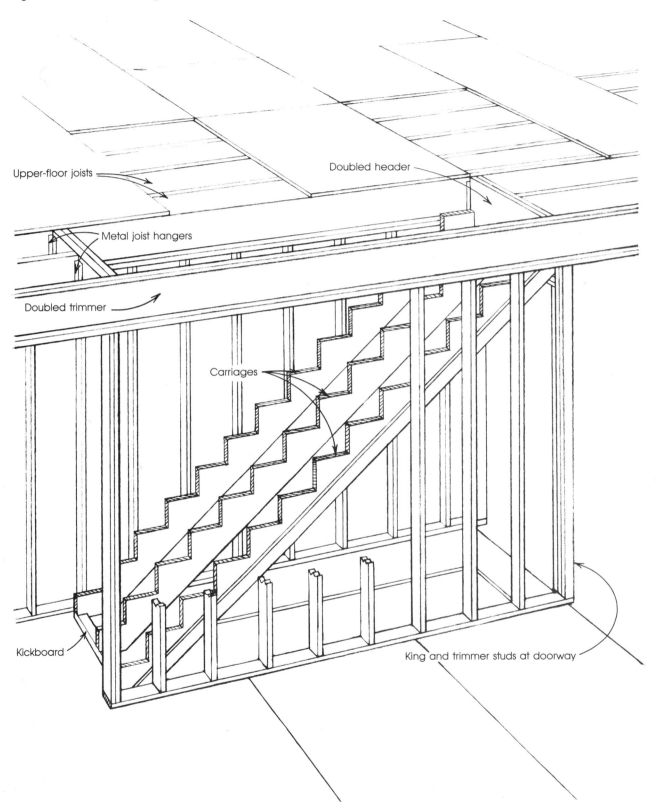

Upper-floor joists

Doubled header

Metal joist hangers

Doubled trimmer

Carriages

Kickboard

King and trimmer studs at doorway

Framing the stairwell opening

Framing the stairwell opening is straightforward once you've decided on its size. Figure 15 shows the framing plan for a typical stairwell.

If the floor joists run parallel to the length of the opening, framing may be as simple as doubling the joists on either side of the opening. A doubled header hung securely between the doubled trimmers frames the width of the opening. Typically, a stairwell is at least 10 ft. long; if it's longer or if upstairs partition walls will bear on the edges of the opening, you should triple the joists or support the well opening with stud walls or posts.

Stairwells in joists that run perpendicular to the opening are more complicated. As shown in Figure 16 on p. 28, the header is still doubled but it must carry the load of a large section of floor. The trimmer joists that define the width of the stairwell are also doubled and carry the load of the doubled header as well. Again, the stairwell may have to be supported from below by a series of posts or stud walls. Figure 16, which shows the order of events in framing, is intended to illustrate the the prin ciples, not necessarily the actual structural members.

The motto of the seat-of-the-pants engineer is "When in doubt, build it stout." Tripling joists and building extra walls may seem to be a waste of lumber, but it's better than having the framing sag or collapse. If you are unsure, I recommend that you contact an engineer or an architect for specific advice on sizing the structural members for your stairwell.

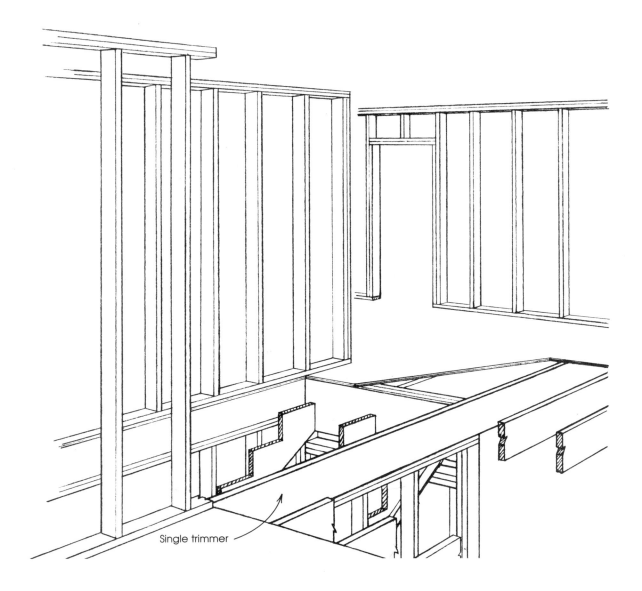

Single trimmer

Figure 16: Stairwell-Opening Order of Events

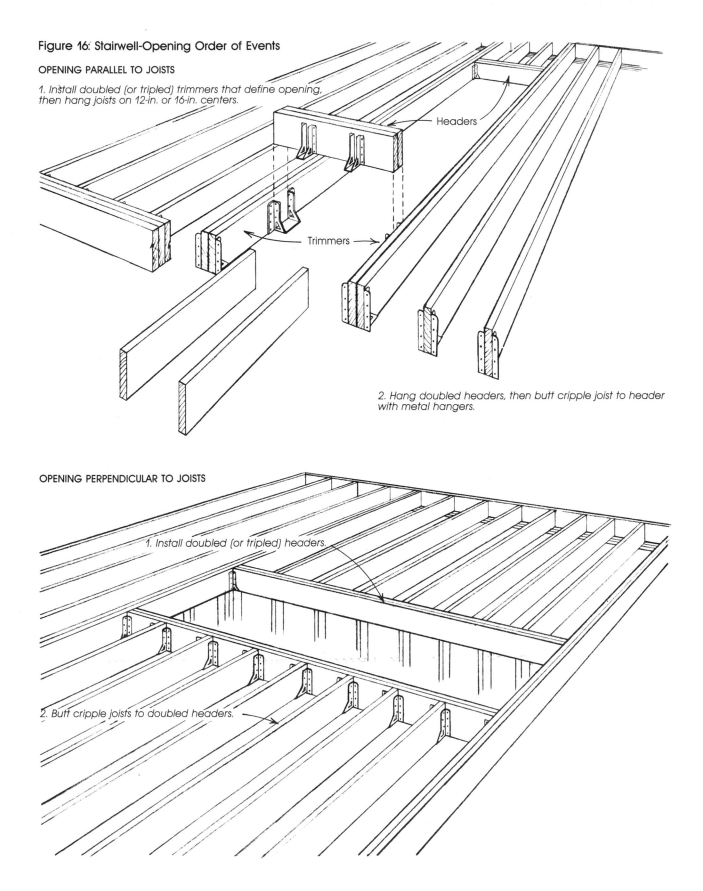

OPENING PARALLEL TO JOISTS

1. Install doubled (or tripled) trimmers that define opening, then hang joists on 12-in. or 16-in. centers.

Headers

Trimmers

2. Hang doubled headers, then butt cripple joist to header with metal hangers.

OPENING PERPENDICULAR TO JOISTS

1. Install doubled (or tripled) headers.

2. Butt cripple joists to doubled headers.

Order of events. The stairwell opening is framed at the same time as the floor system, and as I mentioned, it should be planned for right from the start. Sometimes, in order to save lumber, you might want to place the stairwell opening where the joists naturally fall. This is usually false economy. Let the floor plan, not the framing plan, determine stair location.

Figure 16 shows two typical framing plans, with the stairwell incorporated. If the opening is parallel to the joists, lay out the joists in the usual way (on 16-in. or 12-in. centers). When you reach the stairwell, double (or triple) the joists as shown, but plan to maintain the regular joist spacing. Nail all doubled or tripled joists along their full length, and apply some construction adhesive between the boards.

Once the trimmers are in place, nail the headers across the opening. Since you'll be maintaining the regular joist spacing, some of the otherwise full-length joists will have to be cut and butted to the headers, as shown. If there's no underlying framing, support the cut joists (called cripples) with metal joist hangers, not just end nailing. When installing the decking, extend the plywood just shy of the opening; otherwise, you'll have a miserable time trimming it off later.

Framing stairwells perpendicular to the joists is done in the same way. The trimmer joists, which define the short side of the opening and are doubled or tripled, are installed first just as before. These are full length and are in addition to the joists on the regular layout. The doubled or tripled headers, which are as long as the long dimension of the opening, are installed next. The regular joist layout is transferred to this header from the rim joists, and the cripples that butt to this header are installed last.

If nailing through a header or trimmer into the end of a joist is to be the only support, then you must sequence things so you're not nailing through a doubled beam. Otherwise the nails won't be long enough to penetrate into the end grain. Install the inside trimmers first, then the outside headers, then the cripple joists, then the inside header, and finally the outside trimmer. It's easy to put things in the wrong spot or wrong order, so I prefer to double all the trimmers and headers that define the opening before I put in the cripples. Then use joist hangers wherever there is a butt joint.

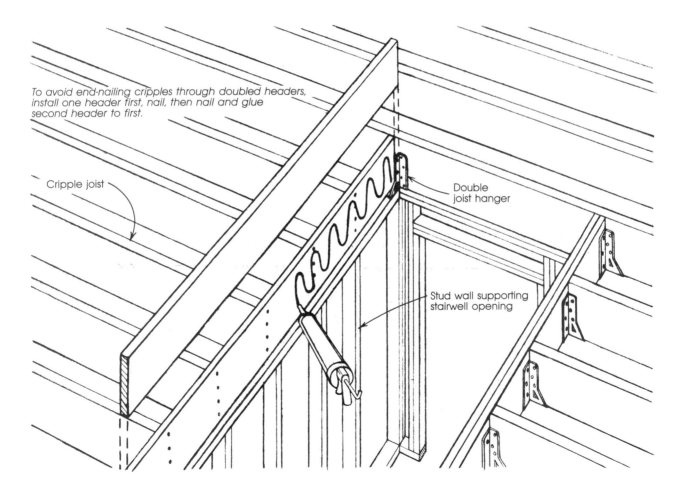

To avoid end-nailing cripples through doubled headers, install one header first, nail, then nail and glue second header to first.

Cripple joist

Double joist hanger

Stud wall supporting stairwell opening

On the straight stair described in this chapter, the plywood treads and risers will be covered with carpet.

A Simple, Straight-Run Stair

Chapter 3

Straight-run stairs are probably the most popular kind of stairs because they're versatile and relatively easy to build. With no landings or switchbacks to complicate construction, a straight stair is a good project on which to learn the basic calculation, layout and framing methods common to all types of stairs, whether they are simple or complex.

As I mentioned in Chapter 1, even a simple straight stair can have several variations. In this chapter I'll elaborate on straight-stair construction and discuss some options we didn't have time to cover in the videotape. I'll focus first on an open cut-carriage stair, with plywood treads and risers that are intended to be covered with carpet. In Chapter 4, I'll show how this stair can be dressed up by substituting oak for the plywood.

Laying out the stair

Beginning a new stair has a bit of the chicken and the egg about it. If your stairwell opening is already built, your stair will have to fit the hole. If not, you'll be able to design the stair you want, and then build the stairwell opening to suit. To keep things simple, I'll assume that the rough framing is in place and that you're standing on the plywood subfloor or on a concrete slab beneath the main level of the house.

First, you'll need to collect some important data, namely, the vertical distance from finished floor to finished floor, or the total vertical rise. With that information in hand, you can use some simple math and the formulas on p. 16 to calculate unit rise and, eventually, total run and unit run (see Figure 17 on p. 32).

To measure total rise accurately, you will have to allow for the thickness of the finished floor, be it hardwood on the main floor, carpet on the second floor or whatever. If you change your mind later about floor covering, the top or bottom unit rise will be incorrect by the difference between what was originally planned and what finally ends up as the finished floor. So think ahead and stick with your decision.

If the upper and lower floors are both to have pad and carpet or the same thickness of hardwood flooring or tile, then the finished-floor to finished-floor dimension will be the same as the subfloor-to-subfloor measurement. But what happens if the lower-level floor is a basement slab and the upper-level floor is to be carpeted? In this case, add the thickness of the pad and carpet to the subfloor-to-subfloor measurement. If, on the other hand, the lower slab gets carpet while the upper-level subfloor gets no additional finished flooring, subtract the carpet thickness from the subfloor-to-subfloor measurement. Figure 18 on p. 32 gives an example.

One last example: the upper floor gets carpet (say ½-in. thickness, total) and the main floor will be ¾-in. thick hardwood. In this situation, you need to add ½ in. to the subfloor-to-subfloor measurement, then subtract ¾ in. to arrive at the finished-floor to finshed-floor dimension. If you happen to have scraps of the finished floor around, you could, of course, put them in place on the subfloors and measure directly.

Measure between subfloors at several points along the stairwell, at all four corners of the opening, for example. Theoretically, both floors will have been framed with care so the measurements should be equal. Sometimes they are not. One floor may be out of level, or there may be a lump of adhesive under the subfloor or perhaps there's a crowned joist in the well opening. Basement slabs are notorious for being out of level. Don't get concerned unless the corners vary by more than ¼ in. A greater error will have to be corrected or compensated for during stair framing. If I can't correct an error, I'll usually pick the shortest vertical distance, then plan to shim under the carriage later to compensate for the low floor.

Figure 17: Figuring Rise and Run

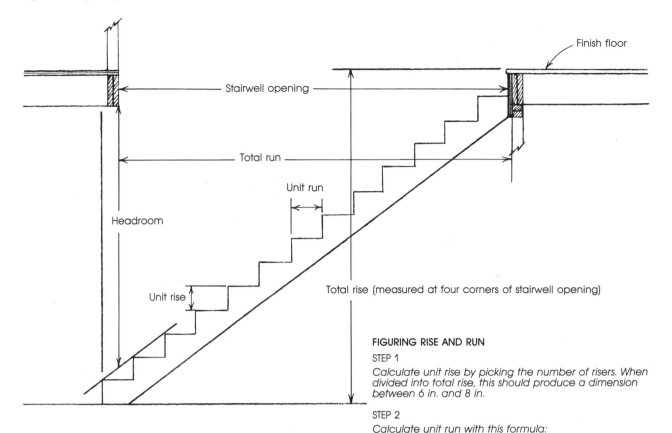

Finish floor

Stairwell opening

Total run

Unit run

Headroom

Unit rise

Total rise (measured at four corners of stairwell opening)

FIGURING RISE AND RUN

STEP 1
Calculate unit rise by picking the number of risers. When divided into total rise, this should produce a dimension between 6 in. and 8 in.

STEP 2
Calculate unit run with this formula:
Unit rise + unit run = 17 in. to 18 in.

STEP 3
Add up unit runs to find total run.

Figure 18: Allowing for Finished Flooring

If finish-floor materials are the same on both levels, then total rise is the subfloor-to-subfloor measurement (107½ in. for sample stair).

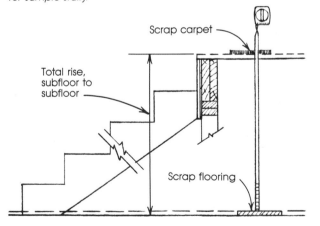

Scrap carpet

Total rise, subfloor to subfloor

Scrap flooring

If flooring materials are of different thicknesses, adjust the subfloor measurement to allow for the finished floor...

...or put scraps of flooring in place and measure directly.

Rise and run. With the total vertical rise in hand, we can use the formulas explained in Chapter 2 to calculate unit rise. At this point, I find it helpful to sketch out a profile view of the stair. This drawing can be to scale, and it should include all elements such as subfloors, finished floors, carriages, the correct number of treads and risers and the method of carriage attachment at the top of the stair. The drawing is also a good place to check for adequate headroom in the stairwell opening, as described on p. 24.

To arrive at unit rise, simply choose a whole number that will divide into the total rise to produce a dimension between 7 in. and 8 in. This number will become the total number of risers. If I decide on 14 risers, for example, and my total vertical rise is 107½ in., I'll end up with a unit rise of $7^{11}/_{16}$ in. This is the rise I demonstrated in the videotape, but let's say the stair I'm building is for an elderly couple and I want a lower rise. Increasing the number of risers to 16 will result in a shallower stair with a unit rise of 6¹¹⁄₁₆ in.

At this point, the sketch I've made helps me keep my thoughts straight on one very important point: the relationship of rise to run and, eventually, of the risers to the treads. Note that the number of unit runs is always one less than the number of unit rises. This is because the total run actually ends where the uppermost and lowermost risers meet the floor. As I experiment with the number of risers, I alter the sketch accordingly, just to keep from getting confused.

Once I have determined the unit rise of the stair, I can calculate the unit run, and then the total run. Using a unit rise of 6¹¹⁄₁₆ in. and knowing that, according to the formula, unit rise plus unit run should total between 17 in. and 18 in., I arrive at a unit run of 10½ in. to 11 in. In this example, I have 16 unit rises and 15 unit runs. Since the total run equals the unit run multiplied by the number of units of run (really the number of treads), my total run for this stair is 157½ in. to 165 in. Once you've settled on total run, add it to your drawing. Use the formula on p. 24 to check headroom.

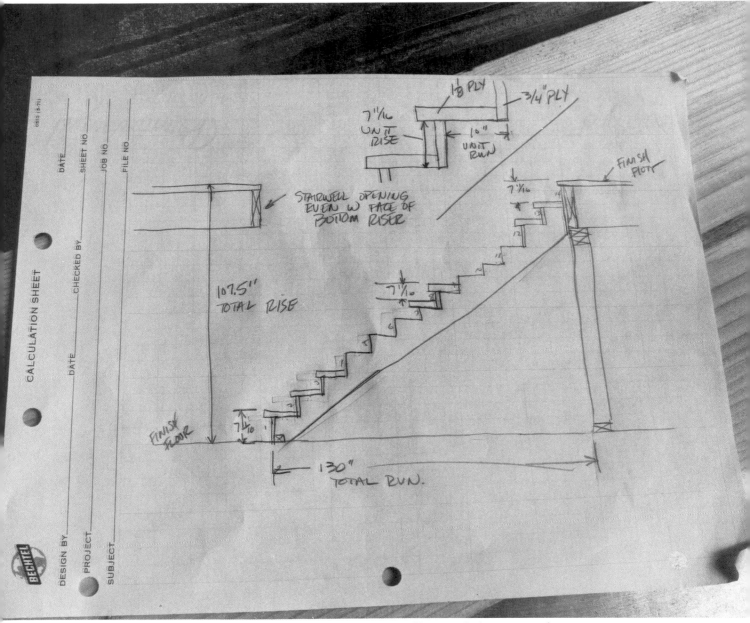

Sketching out the stair to scale clarifies the layout and helps to avoid errors during construction.

Carriage layout. Once I've calculated exact rise and run, I'm ready to lay out and cut the carriages. But first, I need to do one more simple calculation to determine the length of the carriages.

Figure 19 shows how to determine the rough carriage length using the Pythagorean theorem. Note that in the drawing I've added an extra tread at the bottom in order to fill in the triangle. By solving for C, we'll arrive at the approximate length for the stair carriages, plus a little extra to allow for defects in the carriage lumber.

As you might imagine, sound, straight boards are best for carriages. If your carriage boards are warped or crowned or full of knots, you'll have a difficult time building an accurate stair. To ensure myself of good carriage lumber, I "high-grade" my lumber while framing the floors and the roof, which means that I sort through the stack and set aside the best stuff. You can't just order a couple of boards from the lumberyard and expect to get good carriages. If necessary, pick through the pile, even if you must do so over the yardman's objections.

Two-by-twelves are the usual size for carriages. They're wide enough to remain strong after the riser/tread notch has been cut. Most straight-run applications will call for 16-ft. 2x12s. On very short runs or on porch stairs, a 2x10 is acceptable. In Fairbanks, Alaska, where I live, Douglas fir is the usual choice. I'd use hemlock or spruce only if fir wasn't available.

Small, tight knots are acceptable in carriage stock, but large spikes or "bull" knots are not (see Figure 20). If knots are unavoidable, position your layout so they will be removed when the notches are cut. Any large knots that remain should be positioned on the upper edge of the carriage, where they will be in compression, not on the bottom edge, where tension is likely to cause splits around knots. Select only straight boards. Laying out your carriages on crowned lumber guarantees that one car-

Figure 19: Calculating Carriage Length

Since we know total rise (A) and total run (B), calculate C with Pythagorean theorem: $A^2 + B^2 = C^2$.

EXAMPLE:
Total rise is 107½ in., total run is 130 in. (plus 10 in. extra).

$107\frac{1}{2}^2 + 140^2 = 31156.25$

$\sqrt{31156.25} = 176.5$ in., or 14 ft. 8½ in.

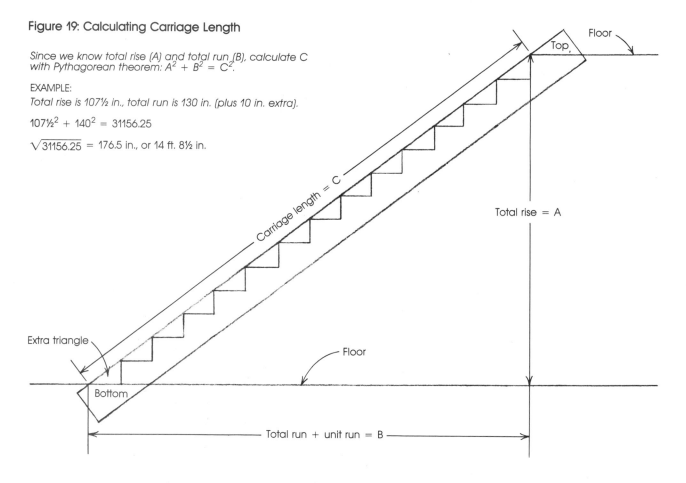

riage will be shorter than the others by an amount large enough to require every tread to be shimmed—a real pain in the neck.

The number of carriages in a stair will be determined by the length of the treads, the materials and thicknesses of the treads and risers and the free span of the carriages. Some building codes require that three carriages be used if the two outer carriages are more than 30 in. apart and the tread thickness is 1 1/16 in., or if the carriages are 36 in. apart with treads 1 1/2 in. thick. This distance is more critical on an open-riser stair, where there are no risers to add stiffness to the structure. I recommend using three carriages as standard stairbuilding practice, unless doing so creates other problems. Sometimes even three carriages won't be enough, and you'll have to install some kind of understair framing to keep the stair from feeling bouncy. One solution to bounciness is to double up the open-side carriage.

Figure 21: Carriage Layout: Two Methods

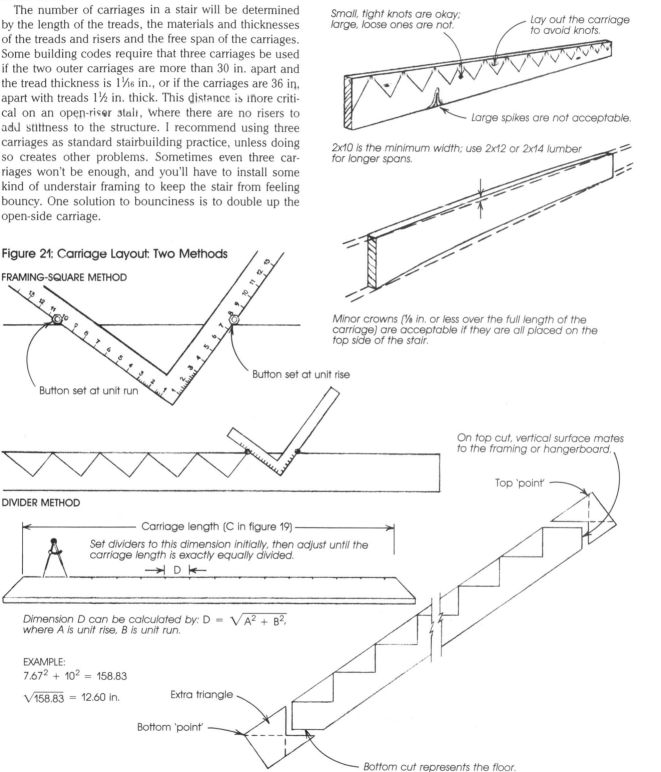

Figure 20: Carriage Lumber

Good carriage lumber is straight, flat and not twisted.

Small, tight knots are okay; large, loose ones are not.

Lay out the carriage to avoid knots.

Large spikes are not acceptable.

2x10 is the minimum width; use 2x12 or 2x14 lumber for longer spans.

Minor crowns (1/8 in. or less over the full length of the carriage) are acceptable if they are all placed on the top side of the stair.

FRAMING-SQUARE METHOD

Button set at unit rise

Button set at unit run

DIVIDER METHOD

Carriage length (C in figure 19)

Set dividers to this dimension initially, then adjust until the carriage length is exactly equally divided.

D

Dimension D can be calculated by: $D = \sqrt{A^2 + B^2}$, where A is unit rise, B is unit run.

EXAMPLE:
$7.67^2 + 10^2 = 158.83$

$\sqrt{158.83} = 12.60$ in.

On top cut, vertical surface mates to the framing or hangerboard.

Top 'point'

Extra triangle

Bottom 'point'

Bottom cut represents the floor.

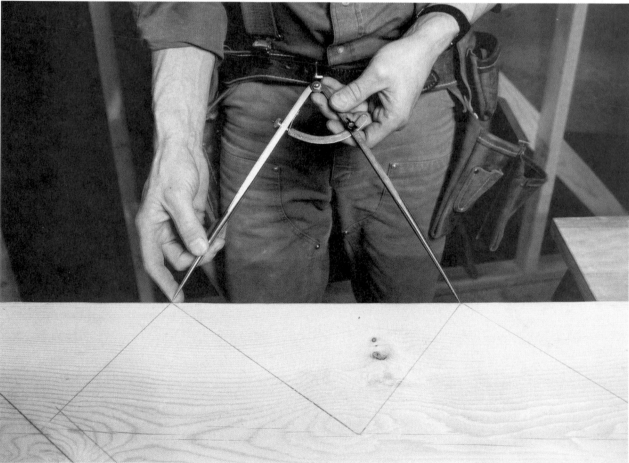

A 1x4 clamped to the square (top) substitutes for stair buttons. Stepping off rise and run cuts with large dividers (above) is another way to lay out the carriage.

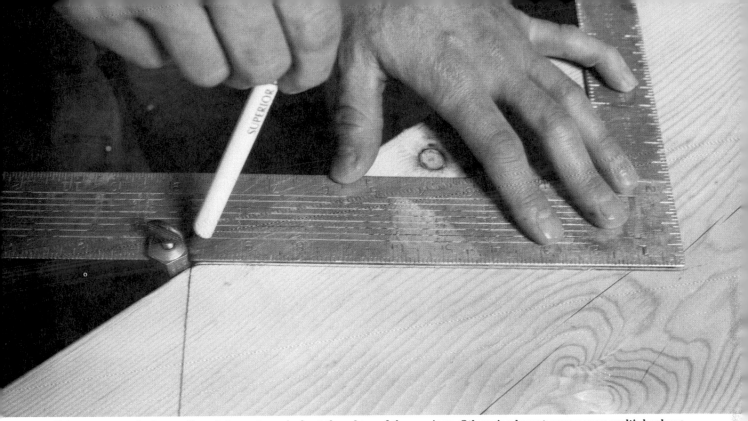

Take care to make layout lines intersect precisely at the edges of the carriage. Otherwise layout errors may multiply along the length of the carriage.

Although some people use it merely as a straightedge, the humble framing square was really invented for tasks like cutting the rise and run notches in stair carriages. To set up the square for this job, use a pair of stair buttons, as shown in Figure 21 on p. 35. The square is positioned so that the edge of the board intersects at the unit rise and unit run. The buttons are then slid snug against the board and tightened down. If you don't have buttons, a 1x4 clamped to the square, as shown in the top photo on the facing page, will work. In any case, use some type of positive guide, not just pencil scratches on the square.

Start at the bottom and mark out lines that represent the unit rise and run, stepping up the board as you go. Most framing lumber has slightly rounded edges that will make it difficult to get a crisp intersection where the layout lines meet, but do the best you can. The slightest inaccuracies will multiply. An error of as little as $\frac{1}{16}$ in. will result in misaligned treads.

Remember that the carriage board is a little longer than required, so go ahead and lay out the extra tread that you added at the bottom. This tread line will actually represent the finished surface of the lower floor. At the top of the carriage, it helps to draw in the last unit rise and the line that would represent the upper finished-floor surface. This last rise and run is not an actual notch in the carriage (see Figure 19 on p. 34), but it will help you visualize the stair and avoid errors.

The measurement between the top and bottom "points" should equal the length you calculated earlier, using the Pythagorean theorem. If it doesn't, it's likely that a small error was introduced at each step. You'll have to go back and make each notch slightly smaller or larger until the total length measurement comes out correctly.

Some carpenters approach carriage layout from a different direction. If you divide the calculated hypotenuse —C in Figure 19 on p. 34—by the total number of steps, you can determine a hypotenuse length for each step. This can be set on a pair of dividers and "stepped off" on the edge of the board, as shown in the bottom photo on the facing page. If you don't end up at the total calculated hypotenuse length, reset the dividers and try again. This is essentially the same principle as the framing-square method, but you don't need to draw lines all over the board until you're sure they're in the right place. Another way of doing the same thing is to use the formula shown in Figure 21 on p. 35.

Dropping the carriage. Now that the carriage is laid out, take a look at the lines you've drawn. The rise and run lines actually represent the finished surface of the risers and treads. If you were to saw your notches to the lines and simply nail the treads on, the top rise would be too small by a dimension equal to the tread thickness. This is because the top riser's corresponding tread is really the

Figure 22: Dropping the Carriage

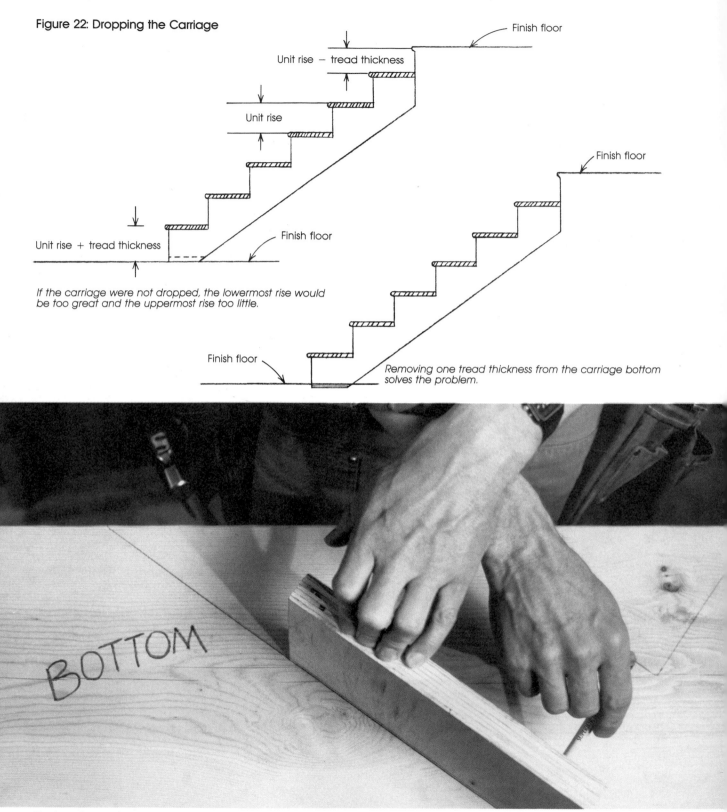

Finish floor

Unit rise − tread thickness

Unit rise

Finish floor

Unit rise + tread thickness

Finish floor

If the carriage were not dropped, the lowermost rise would be too great and the uppermost rise too little.

Finish floor

Finish floor

Removing one tread thickness from the carriage bottom solves the problem.

To drop the carriage, scribe the required cut using a scrap of the actual tread material as a depth gauge. The line above the area labeled 'bottom' represents the finished floor.

finished floor. A tread thickness of a difference in the riser height might not seem like much, but it's enough to cause constant tripping at the top of the stairs.

It would seem logical to fix this is by cutting back from each layout line by an amount equal to the tread thickness, but it's a lot easier to adjust the vertical height of the entire carriage, which automatically corrects all the steps at once. This is known as dropping the carriage, and it's done by trimming the carriage where it meets the finished floor (see Figure 22). In theory, dropping the carriage simply means removing the thickness of one tread from the bottom of the carriage. However, if the thickness of the finish flooring is different at the top and bottom of the stairs or greater or lesser than the tread thickness, you'll have to allow for it.

The important thing to remember is that you want to maintain the correct unit rise from the top of the finished tread to the top of the finished floor. If the finished floor is already in place or carpet will go on both floors, just drop the carriage by an amount equal to the tread thickness. Rather than using a tape to measure this, I find it simplest to grab a scrap of tread material, place it in the correct spot and mark the line, as shown in the photo on the facing page.

Let's say, however, that the finished floor is not in place and that it will be thinner than the treads. In this case, you'll need to calculate the difference between the two thicknesses, then drop the carriage by that dimension. What you're really doing, of course, is dropping the carriage by a tread thickness, then raising it back up to account for the floor thickness. For example, $\frac{3}{4}$-in. thick hardwood flooring will eventually be installed on the subfloor. If the treads are to be $1\frac{1}{8}$-in. hardwood, we'll initially drop the carriage by $1\frac{1}{8}$ in. But to account for the floor, which will be butted up to the bottom riser, we'll have to add $\frac{3}{4}$ in. to the initial drop, for a total net drop of $\frac{3}{8}$ in.

If you're concerned that focusing all your attention at the bottom of the carriage will allow errors to creep in at the top, don't worry. By measuring from finished floor to finished floor, you automatically establish and maintain the correct riser height.

You may, however, need to adjust for the method of attachment to the stairwell opening. Figure 12 on p. 23 shows several approaches. As described in the videotape, I usually use a plywood hangerboard that also serves as the top riser. In laying out the carriage, we took care to make sure that all unit runs—that is, the distance from one vertical cut to the next—were equal.

When the treads and risers are installed, each riser occupies a portion of the horizontal tread cut, but the next riser adds an equal amount to the tread cut above it so the unit rise is maintained. At the top, however, the hangerboard serves as the riser (to be covered later by carpet) and instead of taking up a bit of the notch, it fastens to the end of the carriage. Therefore, to maintain the correct unit run, the end of the carriage must be trimmed back by

the thickness of a riser. You might think of this adjustment as a horizontal version of dropping the carriage.

Carriages that are simply butted to the joists of the stairwell opening, as shown in Figure 12 on p. 23 (note that the cantilevered subfloor forms the top tread), don't have to be adjusted, but you will need a top riser to maintain a constant unit run.

Sawing the carriages. After you have carefully checked your layout lines and marked for the carriage drop, you can saw the notches. I do this with a circular saw and a handsaw. I install a 40-tooth carbide-tipped blade with alternating top-beveled teeth, and I saw very carefully to the waste side of the line. I'm careful not to overshoot the intersection where the tread and riser lines meet. Although some carpenters intentionally overshoot the lines so the waste block will fall clear, I prefer to complete the cut with a handsaw. Overcutting is faster, but it weakens the carriage.

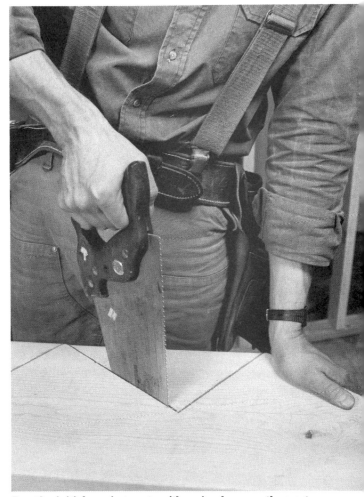

Saw the initial carriage cuts with a circular saw, then cut into the corners with a handsaw.

Before notching the carriages to fit over a 2x4 kickboard nailed to the subfloor, test the fit. Tack the inside carriage to the studs, then check the run cuts for level and the rise cuts for plumb. A 2x4 spacer between the inside carriage and the studs leaves space for the drywall and skirtboard.

Next, lay out and saw the notches for the kickboard, a 2x4 that's nailed to the floor to anchor the bottom of the carriages. Use the first carriage as a template to mark out the other carriages. If the carriage lumber is at all crowned, make sure the crowns are along the top edge of the finished carriages.

Before the cutting the second and third carriages, temporarily install the first carriage to check its fit. Tread cuts should be level and riser cuts plumb, and the carriage should sit flat on the subfloor and against the upper framing or hangerboard. Be sure to check the first and last rise height too. Place scraps of finished flooring and treads in place and make sure that everything checks out. If all is well, go ahead and cut the last two carriages. Don't forget that your layout lines are now totally in the waste side, so take out the lines with your cuts.

Hanging the carriages. Now is a good time to install the hangerboard, if you're using one and it wasn't installed when the stairwell was framed. The hangerboard should be wide enough to support the full width of all three carriages. It shouldn't extend past the bottom of the carriages where it might interfere with the drywall underneath, but it ought to extend up to the underside of the subfloor. Tack it in place, then mark a level horizontal line on the hangerboard at a point that will give you the correct rise when the carriages are installed. Use scraps of finished flooring, if necessary, so you won't forget to allow for the flooring. The hangerboard is made of ¾-in. plywood, which takes nails well and won't split. If you'd prefer other carriage-fastening methods, refer to p. 23.

The tops of the carriages align with a level line marked on the hangerboard. The line is positioned so that the top tread will be one unit rise below the upper-level finished floor.

To illustrate construction more clearly, the stair I built for the videotape is entirely open on one side. Your stair may be the same, or it may have partition walls on both sides. In either case, the main-floor carriages should have structural support—by nailing them directly to the partition wall or, if there is no wall, by constructing underlying framing. I'll explain both methods.

An adjacent wall offers plenty of support for a stair carriage. Carriages can be nailed directly to the studs, but the drywall and skirtboard would then have to be notched, sawtooth fashion, around the carriage. This amounts to a lot of extra work, and worse, it radically reduces the area where the treads bear against the carriage run cuts. This makes it difficult to screw or nail plywood treads, and it is unacceptable for hardwood treads.

The solution is to leave a space between the wall-side carriage and the studs, as shown in the photo above right and on the videotape. The drywall and skirtboard can then be slid into this space. I usually leave a 1½-in. space, which leaves plenty of room for a ¾-in. skirt and ½-in. or ⅝-in. drywall. If you're going to panel the wall, adjust the space to suit. I create the 1½-in. space by nailing a 2x4 diagonally to the studs at the same angle as the carriage. The carriage is then nailed to the 2x4 spacer.

To mark the studs for the spacer, place the carriage against the wall in its proper position, then mark each stud along the bottom edge of the carriage, as shown in the photo below left. Hold the bottom edge of the spacer to these lines and drive two nails into each stud through the spacer. If the stair is closed, the carriage on the opposite partition wall is handled in the same way.

Install the outside carriages first by placing one or the other in the correct position and tacking it temporarily. Check for alignment with the line on the hangerboard and with your wall spacer. If everything looks okay, tack the other outside carriage in place, then install the third carriage, centered between the outer carriages. Set the bottom of the carriages the correct distance apart, then cut and install the kickboard.

At this point, check all three carriages and make sure the run cuts are level and the rise cuts plumb. A level placed across the carriages will detect any horizontal or vertical misalignments. Check each step. Small errors, of say $1/16$ in., are no problem but larger ones will have to corrected, usually by bringing the problem carriage into line with a shim placed between it and the subfloor.

Once the fit of the carriages proves satisfactory, you can go ahead and nail the carriages permanently in position. Nail through the back of the hangerboard into the carriages with 16d nails. Metal joist hangers can be added for some extra insurance, as shown in the photo on p. 44. Nail through the sides of the carriages into the spacer, also with 16d nails, and then toenail the carriages into the kickboard.

Mark for the spacer by scribing lines on the studs under the inner carriage, then nail on the spacer. Check the carriage fit one last time, then nail the carriages through the back of the hangerboard to the studs and to the kickboard. The middle carriage should be centered between the two outer carriages.

Although not absolutely necessary, metal joist hangers strengthen the carriage-to-hangerboard joint.

Once the carriages have been nailed firmly in place, you will need to install some blocking between the studs at points where drywall, skirts or railing will be anchored. This blocking is nothing more than short scraps of 2x4. See Figure 23 for information on how the blocking should be installed.

The outside carriage of an open stair is handled a little differently. Since there's no wall to support the outside carriage, supporting framing must be built underneath the carriage (see Figure 24) or the carriage must be doubled up. Tack the wall-side carriage in place first, then position the outside carriage and tack it in place.

Figure 23: Blocking

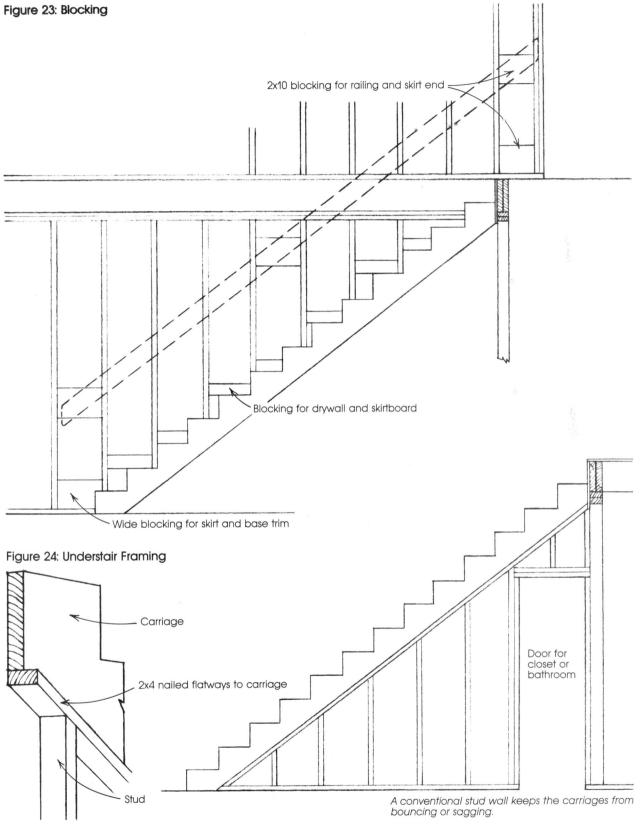

2x10 blocking for railing and skirt end

Blocking for drywall and skirtboard

Wide blocking for skirt and base trim

Figure 24: Understair Framing

Carriage

2x4 nailed flatways to carriage

Stud

Door for closet or bathroom

A conventional stud wall keeps the carriages from bouncing or sagging.

Figure 25: Tread and Riser Design

Nosing overhang equals the tread thickness.

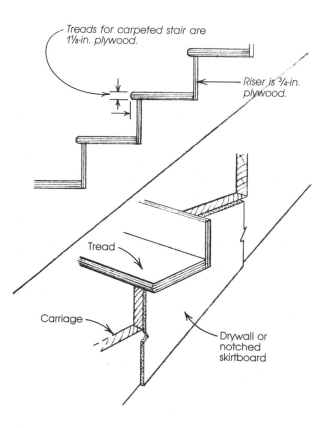

Treads for carpeted stair are 1⅛-in. plywood.

Riser is ¾-in. plywood.

Tread

Carriage

Drywall or notched skirtboard

Treads to be carpeted can overhang the carriage...

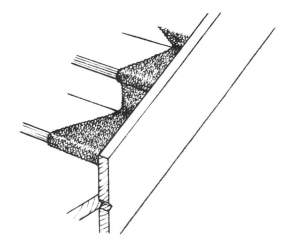

...or butt to a skirtboard without sawn notches.

Treads and risers. Now that the carriages are in place, you can move on to the treads and risers, the elements that give a stair its walking surfaces. Long before making and installing them, you will have made some fundamental design decisions about the treads and risers. In this case, we'll be carpeting the stair so the treads will be plywood; even at that, there are several ways to design them (see Figure 25). In Chapter 4, I'll describe how to install oak or other hardwood treads and risers.

A carpeted stair that's closed on both sides is the easiest to deal with. The plywood treads and risers are simply butted to the skirtboards and nailed down. The carpet covers all, hiding any minor gaps between the ends of the treads and risers and the skirtboards.

A carpeted open stair is a little trickier to deal with. The simplest (but in my opinion least attractive) approach is to let the treads and risers overhang the carriage by about 1½ in. The drywall is installed on the outside face of the rough carriage so that it just butts to the overhanging treads and risers. The carpet is then wrapped around these overhangs. Carpet installers call this "upholstery work," and it makes their eyes light up because it's usually billed at an hourly rate.

A better design is to add a finished skirtboard, which is basically a trim-quality board (say, pine or poplar) cut to the same sawtooth pattern as the rough carriage. The carpet then wraps the tread as before and butts to the skirtboard. It's not much different technically, but it makes a big improvement visually.

Another version of the skirtboard is a board without notches installed over the ends of the treads and risers. This can be called an open stair with a closed skirt or stringer. Here the carpet butts to both the inside and outside skirtboard. To look right, the skirt should be at least 1 in. thick. This closed skirt will also provide a convenient place to anchor balusters, which would otherwise have to butt into the treads. (More on railings later, in Chapter 5.)

At this point, I'm ready to make my treads and risers. For the carpeted stairway in the videotape, I used 1⅛-in. underlayment-grade plywood for the treads and ¾-in. plywood for the risers. This stair has a unit run of 10 in. and a nosing of 1⅛ in., which allows the tread to overhang the riser below it by 1⅛ in., as shown in Figure 25.

Adding the nosing to the unit run gives me a total tread width of 11⅛ in. The nosing itself is a radiused or chamfered upper edge on each tread. It can be made with a radius bit or a chamfering bit on a router. The purpose of nosing is to keep the carpet from having to make a hard turn around the sharp front edges of the treads, which would expose the backing to premature wear. Don't forget to round over the tread and riser ends if the carpet will wrap around them.

The risers are ripped to a width slightly less than the unit rise, which is 7¹¹⁄₁₆ in. in this case. I cut the risers a hair narrow so I don't have to fuss with fits later on. After

Treads for a carpeted stair are made of 1⅛-in. plywood. Rip the treads to width on a table saw and crosscut them to length (left). Then round over the nosing with a router (right).

Before the treads and risers are installed, notch the upper subfloor to receive the skirtboard. The notch depth should extend to the face of the top riser, which is actually the hangerboard in this photo.

all, any minor gaps will be covered with carpet anyway. Note that the bottom riser is narrower than the others by the width of one tread, because it doesn't have to lap another tread. Note also that there really is no top riser; the hangerboard serves this function.

The upper plywood subfloor, which was left long, should be trimmed back to have the same nosing overhang as the other treads. Don't forget to round it over with the router. At this point, you should also saw a small notch in the plywood subfloor nearest the closed side of the stairway. This notch will receive the skirtboard. The notch should go all the way back to the face of the hanger, which serves as the top riser and also the point where the skirt terminates. Again, there's no need for a perfect fit, as the carpet will cover minor gaps.

I rip all the treads and risers to width first (remember that the bottom riser is narrower than the rest), then crosscut them to length. If you have a table saw or a radial-

Because the carriage is dropped one tread thickness, the bottom riser is narrower than the rest.

arm saw, set it up with a stop for repetitive cuts to length. The length should be such that the tread is flush with the outside carriage (or overhanging it, if you prefer) while leaving enough space for the drywall and skirtboard between the studs and the inside carriage. Don't make the clearance too tight, however. Remember, the carpeting will cover minor gaps.

I like to glue and screw or nail the treads and risers. Glue keeps the stair from popping and squeaking, and it ties everything together, which makes the stair stronger. I use plenty of construction adhesive wherever a tread or riser meets the carriages. I also spread a bead of adhesive on the top of each riser as a bed for the next tread, and on the back of each tread where it laps the next riser. An average-size stair will consume two large tubes of adhesive. Rather than latex-type adhesive, I prefer the smellier solvent-base adhesives. These are also flammable, so be careful when using them.

Install the first and second riser first, then the bottom tread. Apply construction adhesive to the backs of the treads and risers, then screw them to the carriages with drywall screws.

To minimize squeaks and creaks, drive screws through the backs of each riser into the edges of the treads.

Begin by stacking the risers and treads near the stair, along with all the tools you'll need, including nails, hammer, screws and electric screwdriver. I start at the bottom of the stair by installing two risers, then fill in between with a tread. As shown in the photo at left on p. 50, spread a bead of adhesive on the back of each riser, and then tack it in place with 8d finish nails. When you're satisifed with the fit, drive 2¼-in. drywall screws through the risers into the carriage. Don't be afraid to use two or three screws per side. I predrill the treads and riser so they'll pull up tight against the carriage, but you don't need to bore pilot holes in the carriage itself.

With two risers in place, install the first tread, gluing the back as before and driving screws when the tread is properly positioned. I drive screws through the top of each tread down into the carriage below and from the back of each riser into the edges of the treads. Here, a pilot hole is a good idea. It will keep the screws from splitting the plywood laminations. If the underside of the stair has already been drywalled it's still possible to get at these back screws by using a drill with a right-angle drive. On the whole, though, it's better to build the stair before drywalling the underside.

As you install the treads and risers, check to see that each one mates accurately with the carriages. The carriages probably won't align perfectly, either because of minor layout errors or twists in the floor and framing. If this is so, slip small shims to take up any gaps between the treads and risers and the carriages. Be sure to set the shims in a generous bed of adhesive.

Trimming the stair

Once the treads and risers have been installed, the stair should be trimmed out and made ready for carpet. For this simple stair, trimming consists of adding a skirtboard and installing the rails. Before the trimwork is done, hang the drywall, tape the joints and paint.

A skirtboard isn't absolutely necessary but will protect the drywall against damage from shoes, and it's a nice wood accent that gives the stair a finished touch. Skirtboards also tie in the stair with other trim in the house, especially the baseboard, base cap and shoe moldings.

For the skirtboard on this stair, I picked a clear fir 1x10. One-by-ten is about the minimum width for a skirt, which must at the very least fill the tread/riser triangles and extend past the tread nosing by about 2¼ in. This amount of projection ensures that the skirtboard will look right and that it will mate correctly to the baseboard.

I usually lay out the skirtboard by measuring the stair and then transferring these measurements directly to the skirtboard. First, measure out from the tread nosing near the bottom and the top of the stair, as shown in Figure 26. To find the skirt's total length, hook your tape to a nail driven in the lower-level floor and measure to the top of the stairs. Cut the skirt a little long, then trim it to fit.

The skirt's top edge can be left square, eased over with a router or molded to match the other trim. Figure 26 shows how the skirt can be tied into the surrounding trim. Nail the skirt in place or fasten it with screws and plugs, then apply a couple of coats of varnish or paint.

Figure 26: Skirtboard Detail

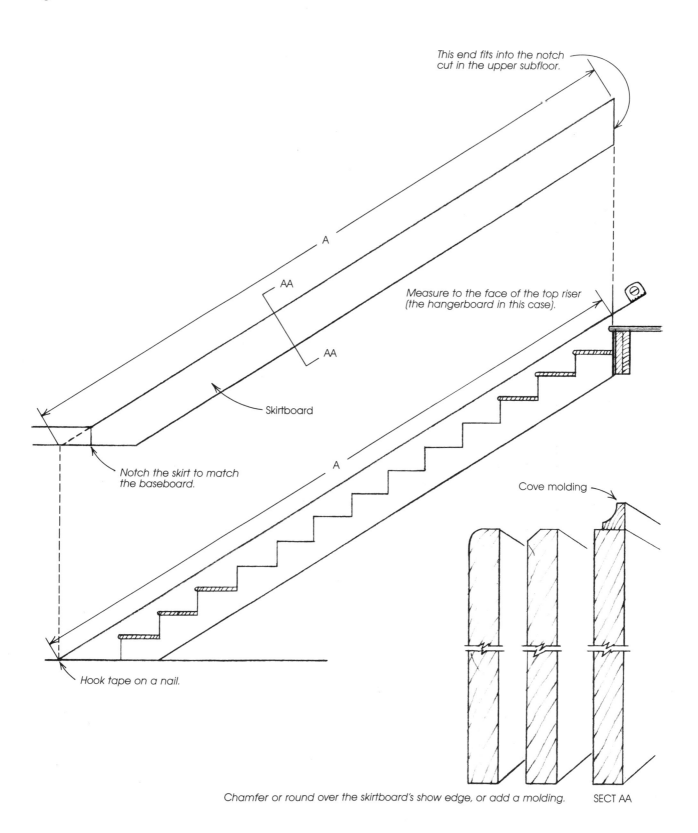

This end fits into the notch cut in the upper subfloor.

A

AA

AA

Measure to the face of the top riser (the hangerboard in this case).

Skirtboard

Notch the skirt to match the baseboard.

A

Hook tape on a nail.

Cove molding

Chamfer or round over the skirtboard's show edge, or add a molding.

SECT AA

The stair half completed, with the uppermost treads and risers left off to show the relationship of the skirtboard and drywall to the wall-side carriage.

Handrailing for a closed stair is fairly simple. Both walls enclosing the stair can support a rail An open stair could get a railing on both the wall side and the open side. (For more on open-stair railings, see Chapter 5.) On closed stairs, you can install the stock pine or oak railing most lumberyards sell, using garden-variety metal brackets. Or, as I prefer to do, you can make up your own railing out of fir or pine and mount it on small wooden spacers, as shown in Figure 27.

Off-the-shelf metal brackets are remarkably durable, provided they are screwed solidly into backing and not fastened to the drywall with molly bolts. Shopmade railings should be made of 1¼-in. thick fir, pine, oak or whatever wood matches the stair. The rail should be at least 3 in. wide, with a plumb cut on both ends. Don't try to get away with a ¾-in. board. It violates code, looks anemic and isn't thick enough to grip comfortably. With a router, round over the top and bottom edges of the rail. As shown in Figure 27, the rail is held away from the wall with 1½-in. blocks, providing ample room for the knuckles.

Figure 27: Shopmade Rail

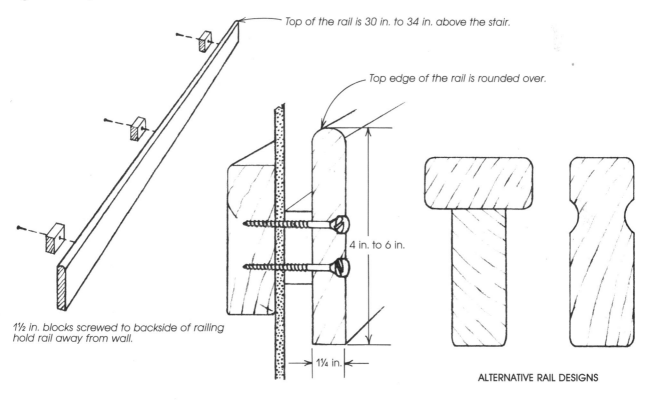

Top of the rail is 30 in. to 34 in. above the stair.

Top edge of the rail is rounded over.

4 in. to 6 in.

1¼ in.

1½ in. blocks screwed to backside of railing hold rail away from wall.

ALTERNATIVE RAIL DESIGNS

Schuttner's L-shaped stair is built with oak treads and risers and a traditional housed stringer.

An L-Shaped Stair: Skirts, Treads and Risers

Chapter 4

When most people talk about a "traditional" stair, they're thinking of one with oak treads and risers and a full balustrade, complete with molded or turned balusters and newel posts. This style of construction is considered by many to be the height of the stairbuilder's craft and definitely a step above cut-carriage work. In this chapter, I'll describe how a traditional stair is built, using an L-shaped stair as my example.

I picked an L-shape for several reasons. As I explained in Chapter 1, an L-shaped stair is ideal when floor space is tight because it can be tucked into a corner. Even when space isn't a concern, an L-shaped stair is more visually appealing than a straight case, and the landing provides a logical spot for a window, whose natural light adds interest. Since an L-shaped stair has such aesthetic appeal to begin with, it makes sense to build to a higher standard of construction.

Although it's not necessarily harder to build than a straight case, an L-shaped stair does require careful planning. Instead of simply screwing and nailing the case as with the carpeted stair, each tread/riser unit is "joined" by housing it in a mortise and locking it in place with glued wedges. On the stair's open side, the risers are mitered to the skirtboard, and each tread is joined to its riser with a tongue-and-groove joint.

I have chosen to apply these joinery methods to an L-shaped stair, but they could just as easily be used to build a straight stair. In the same way, the cut-carriage method explained in Chapter 3 could also be applied to an L-shaped stair. Throughout this chapter, I'll describe options to simplify construction. These will usually involve the elimination of some joinery, but the stair will retain the same overall look.

Stairwell and landing

Because the stair makes a 90° turn as it ascends, we must allow space for the landing platform when laying out the stairwell. It's easiest to think of the platform as an extra-wide tread that separates what would otherwise be a straight-run stair into two smaller runs. As such, the landing will figure in the rise and run calculations, but to figure overall stairwell size we must first determine the overall dimensions of the landing.

Figuring the landing size. We begin by deciding on the stair width. For this stair, I chose the code minimum of 36 in., measured in this case from the inside face of the wall-side skirtboard to the centerline of the balustrade, as shown in Figure 28 on p. 58. The balustrade serves as a reference point because it represents a common axis for parts of varying width, like balusters, newels and handrails. I should point out that the dimensions I'm calculating here apply only to this particular stair. I recommend that you use the method described to arrive at dimensions for whatever numbers fit the stair you're building.

To find the long dimension of the landing, that is, the dimension that is perpendicular to the lower flight of stairs, measure out from the studs on the closed side. To the basic stair width of 36 in., add 1¼ in. for the housed stringer and ½ in. for the drywall, yielding a total dimension of 37¾ in. from the studs to the centerline of the balustrade. To this, add the offset between the centerline of the balustrade and the face of the lower flight's vertical cut, ¾ in. in this case. Then add the foot of the cut carriage, which is 9¾ in. This gives a total of 48¼ in. for the landing length.

Figure 28: Measuring and Laying Out the Landing

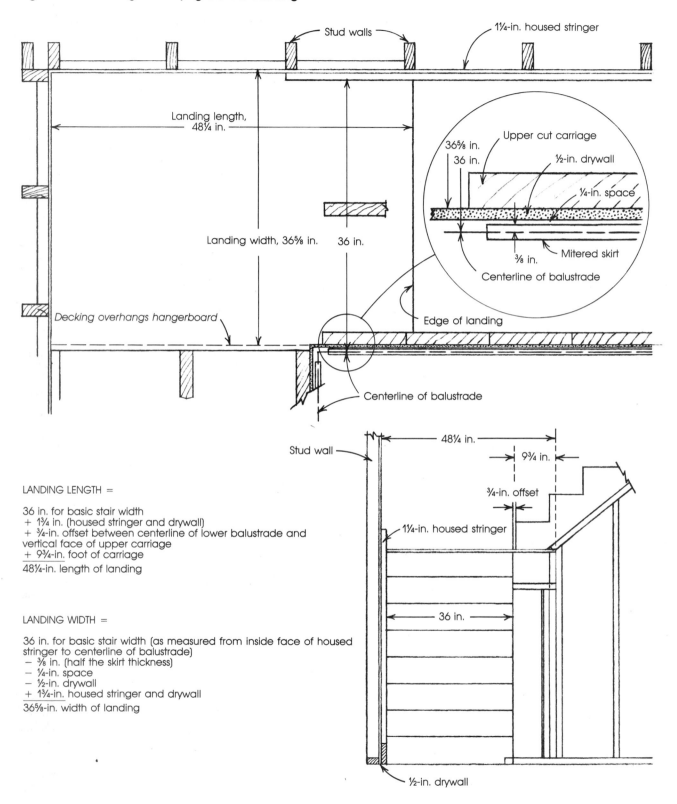

Stud walls

1¼-in. housed stringer

Landing length, 48¼ in.

36⅝ in.
36 in.

Upper cut carriage

½-in. drywall

¼-in. space

Landing width, 36⅝ in.

36 in.

⅜ in.

Mitered skirt

Centerline of balustrade

Decking overhangs hangerboard

Edge of landing

Centerline of balustrade

Stud wall

48¼ in.

9¾ in.

¾-in. offset

1¼-in. housed stringer

36 in.

½-in. drywall

LANDING LENGTH =

36 in. for basic stair width
+ 1¾ in. (housed stringer and drywall)
+ ¾-in. offset between centerline of lower balustrade and vertical face of upper carriage
+ 9¾-in. foot of carriage
48¼-in. length of landing

LANDING WIDTH =

36 in. for basic stair width (as measured from inside face of housed stringer to centerline of balustrade)
− ⅜ in. (half the skirt thickness)
− ¼-in. space
− ½-in. drywall
+ 1¾-in. housed stringer and drywall
36⅝-in. width of landing

The width of the landing—that is, the dimension parallel to the lower flight—is determined by the relationship between the outside face of the upper cut carriage and the centerline of the upper balustrade. The centerline of the balustrade is vertically aligned with the mitered-skirt centerline, as shown in Figure 28. The edge of the landing is flush with this outside face, and, since we know the distance from the studs to the centerline (calculated above), all we have to do is subtract the distance from the centerline to the face of the carriage. For this particular stair, here's how the math works out: 36 in. for the basic stair width plus 1¾ in. for the housed stringer and drywall on the closed side. From this total (37¾ in.), subtract ⅜ in. for half the thickness of the skirt and ¾ in. for drywall and a space between the skirt and the cut carriage. This gives a total of 36⅝ in. for the landing width.

The finished height of the landing will be a multiple of the calculated unit rise, which, as in Chapter 3, is figured from the total rise from finish floor to finish floor. Note that I said "finished height" of the landing. The landing may have flooring that's of a different thickness hardwood from that used for the treads, and we'll have to account for this difference when calculating platform height.

Let's assume the same total rise used in Chapter 3: 107½ in., subfloor to subfloor. Let's further assume that ½-in. carpet will be laid on the ground and second floor, so the finished-floor to finished-floor dimension will also be 107½ in. Our unit rise of 7¹¹⁄₁₆ in. and unit run of 10 in.

are also the same. I've located the landing's finished floor 7 unit rises (exactly half the total rise) up from the lower finished floor, which is itself ½ in. above the subfloor. This makes the finished height of the landing 54¼ in. above the subfloor. Since there will be oak flooring on the landing, I need to lower my landing's subfloor by ¾ in., then drop it another ¾ in. for the plywood subfloor on the landing, for a final height of 52¾ in. to the top of the landing's framing.

Figuring the stairwell size. Now that the platform dimension is known, we can use it to calculate the stairwell size, assuming, of course, that the well isn't already in place. To arrive at the stairwell size, we'll need to allow for run in two directions, one to figure out the well width, the other the well length. This is explained in general terms in Chapter 2 and in greater detail below.

First, let's figure the well length, the dimension that runs parallel to the upper flight. Since we've already determined the length of the platform and we know where the upper flight will rest on it, we can proceed from there. We split total rise into 7 units each for the upper and lower flight. If we were using the hangerboard method described in Chapter 3, this would equate to 6 unit runs, or 60 in. of total run. However, I've added an extra tread on the upper flight, which will overlap the plywood subfloor for a total run of 70 in. The top tread doesn't really need to be a full 10 in. (it's really part of the upper floor),

LANDING HEIGHT

7¹¹⁄₁₆ in. × 7 (number of unit rises) = 53¾ in. to top of landing finish floor from main finish floor

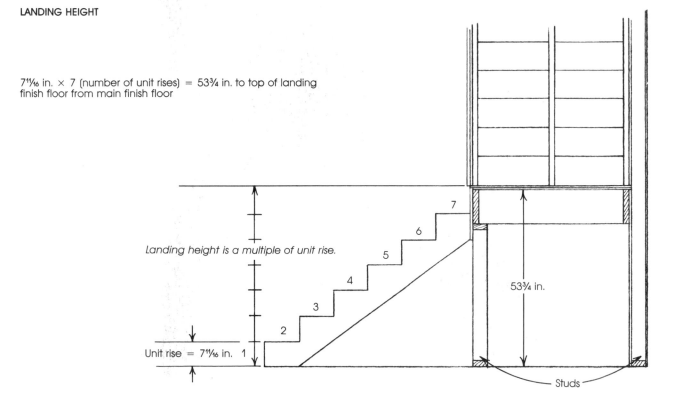

Landing height is a multiple of unit rise.

Unit rise = 7¹¹⁄₁₆ in.

53¾ in.

Studs

Figure 29: Landing Framing Plan

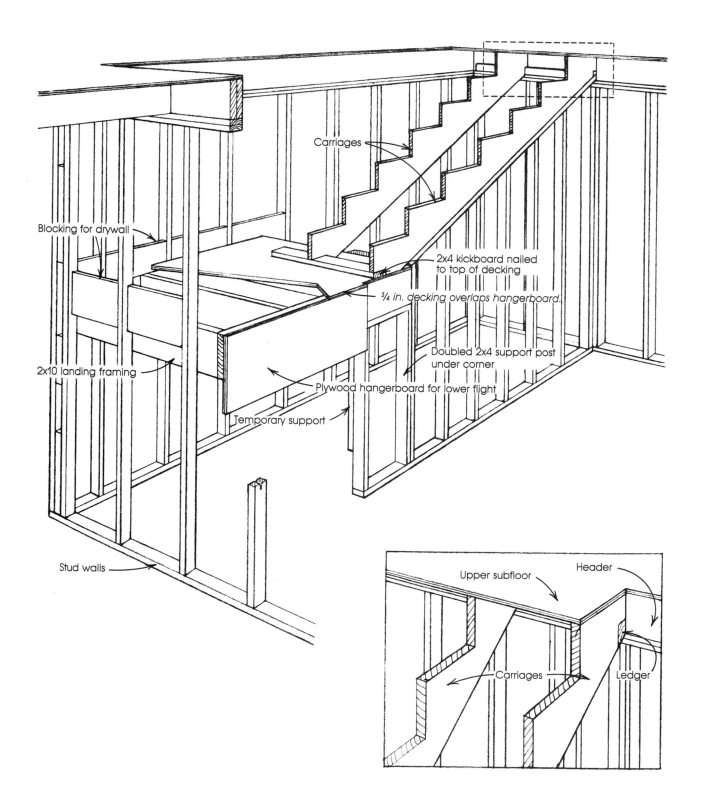

Carriages

Blocking for drywall

2x4 kickboard nailed
to top of decking

¾ in. decking overlaps hangerboard.

2x10 landing framing

Doubled 2x4 support post
under corner

Plywood hangerboard for lower flight

Temporary support

Stud walls

Upper subfloor

Header

Carriages

Ledger

so I've reduced the total run to 68 in. If I need to fudge a little later on, the top tread can be lengthened or shortened as necessary.

The upper run (68 in.) is measured from the vertical cut of the bottom carriage to the edge of the stairwell framing. To arrive at the total stairwell-opening length, add to this dimension the distance from the stud wall to the upper carriage's vertical face, In this case, 38½ in., for a total stairwell opening length of 106¼ in.

After this tortuous routine, figuring stairwell width is easy. Just add the landing width to the run of the lower stair, with one minor adjustment. For the lower flight, we'll be using a hangerboard, nailed right to the landing framing. Since the hanger won't double as a finished riser as in our straight-run stairs, its thickness will need to be added to the run of the stairs. In this case, a landing width of 36⅝ in. plus 60 in. for the lower stair's run plus ¾ in. for the hangerboard totals 97⅜ in. for the stairwell width. If the stairwell framing is to be covered by drywall, add a little extra and round off to the next largest inch for a final stairwell opening of 107 in. by 98 in.

This particular stairwell is a large rectangle to allow for a balcony overlooking the stairway and a grand two-story view upward. A design like this really eats up a lot of floor space. In a smaller house, the stairwell could be an L-shaped hole, which would still use our calculated dimensions for its long-side measurements. You'd then pick a width for the hole using the same considerations as presented on pp. 31-33 for calculating stairwell size for straight-run stairs.

Framing the stairwell follows the normal principles of joist and header construction. Since our stairwell opening is a little over 8 ft. by 9 ft., there's no advantage in orienting it with or across the joists. You'll need a doubled header around the perimeter of the opening, and to avoid heavy beams, the spans should be supported by partition walls or posts at the corners of the opening, as described in Chapter 2.

Framing the landing. The framing of the landing is straightforward. It can be built in place, board by board, or be pre-assembled and installed as a unit. In the stair shown in the videotape, I built the landing in place, mainly because the camera crew couldn't help me lift a pre-assembled landing. Figure 29 shows the framing plan for the landing.

The landing platform will be nailed to a level line scribed on both stud walls.

I prefer to build the landing before the drywall is hung but it can be done afterwards, although this tends to make it more difficult to install supporting framing. For this stair, I nailed the landing to the studs on two walls, leaving one unsupported corner that required a post. Usually this post is incorporated into the wall framing that closes off a part or all of the underside of the stairs. If you're nailing the platform to an outside wall, don't forget to install a vapor barrier.

The lower understairs area is not very large, and a wall closing it off looks better than a single freestanding post. By closing off the area under both flights, you can create a large closet or perhaps a small bathroom. You should also check your local code. Some codes require that stair enclosures be protected against fire by a wall rated for two hours to keep fire from burning through the support structure and blocking exit. In any case, it's nice to be able to get at the underside of the stairs during construction, so save the drywall work until last. If you're building a closet, you won't have to drywall beneath the steps.

Place the joists of the landing on the same centers as the main-floor framing. Be sure to provide support for the center carriage of the upper flight, so that its foot is not resting on plywood alone. If the underside of the platform is not closed off, you'll be able to add blocking as the need arises. I allow the plywood subfloor to overhang the front edge of the landing by ¾ in., so that it flushes up with the hangerboard and creates a tight joint.

Once joists have been nailed in (above), the landing is decked and the hangerboard is installed (below).

Installing the carriages

Once the landing is in place, we can cut and install the upper and lower carriages. These are really just two short straight runs with identical unit rise and unit run, so the carriage-making methods described on pp. 34-37 will work here too. The carriage-dropping method will be a little different, however. And you'll need only two carriages per flight (for a total of four) because the treads and risers on the closed side of this stair will be let into a housed stringer, not supported by a carriage.

Before marking out the carriages, I double-check the height of the installed landing. If there's a mistake, I want to know about it before I saw good lumber into carriages. For this stair, the unit rise is $7^{11}/_{16}$ in. and the unit run 10 in., the same as for the straight stair in Chapter 3.

Using the layout method described earlier, I lay out and saw the cut carriages, using one carriage as a template for the other three. When dropping the carriage, consider the material to be used on the lower floor. In this case, I'll have ½ in. of carpet on the lower floor, 1⅛-in. thick oak treads and ¾-in. thick oak flooring on the landing. The oak flooring doesn't affect the carriage drop because I allowed for it when I calculated the landing height. So the drop for the lower flight will be 1⅛ in. for the tread thickness, minus ½ in. for the carpet—a drop of ⅝ in. Because the hangerboard won't double as a riser, we don't have to subtract its thickness from the carriage length.

Figure 30: Measuring Actual Run

Adjust upper carriage length by measuring the actual run available, not the calculated run.

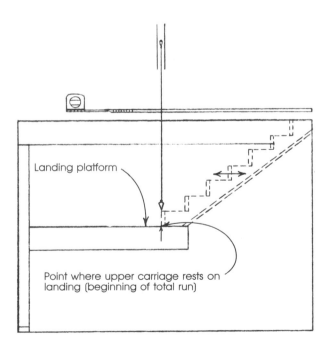

Landing platform

Point where upper carriage rests on landing (beginning of total run)

Lay out and cut one carriage, then use it as a template for laying out the other three.

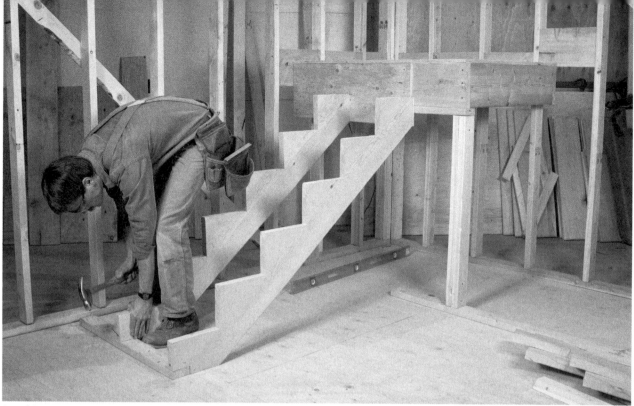

As with the straight stair, the lower carriages are nailed to a kickboard on the floor and, at the landing, to a hanger-board that's notched to accept the newel post.

The lower flight. At this point, you go ahead and install the lower flight. First, nail on the lower hangerboard. The hangerboard's length should be equal to the distance between the outer carriage and the stud wall, or $36\frac{5}{8}$ in. in this case, as shown in Figure 28 on p. 58. If you look closely at the photo at left, you'll note that the hanger is notched. I'll go into more detail about this later, but for now, keep in mind that this notch mates to a corresponding notch in the landing newel post, giving the post a firm vertical purchase. The notch can be cut before or after the hanger is installed. Notch both lower carriages for a kickboard, then nail them in place through the hangerboard and to the ground floor.

The upper flight. The upper flight is constructed in a similar way. However, we do have to allow for the landing's oak floor, which isn't yet in place. So drop the carriage $1\frac{1}{8}$ in. for the tread thickness, then add $\frac{3}{4}$ in. for the flooring, for a net drop of $\frac{3}{8}$ in. All of the unit runs are the same except for the top tread. Here we'll need to measure the actual horizontal distance available to us, not the size it was, in theory, supposed to be.

To do this, mark where the top carriages will rest on the landing. Then, with a plumb bob, plumb up to the plane of the top floor and measure horizontally, as shown in Figure 30 on p. 63. Any small discrepancies can be adjusted by making the last tread a little longer or shorter. Otherwise, errors would have to be fixed by repositioning the carriages on the landing, a method bound to ripple the error all the way to the bottom flight.

There's one other thing to consider. When we dropped the carriage, we lowered it so that the top tread cut would be 1⅛ in. below the upper finished floor surface. However, because the carpet is not yet in place, this finished surface is actually ½ in. above the plywood. Add to that the ¾-in. thickness of the plywood and you'd have to lower the carriage 1¼ in. just to fit it under the overhanging subfloor. You don't want to alter the carriage drop, so you'll have to trim ⅛ in. off the horizontal or run cut.

As shown in the photos above and at right, both the top and bottom of the upper carriages are notched. The bottom notch fits over a kickboard, while the tops of the carriages fit around a ledger nailed to the stairwell header. To allow for drywall, the bottom edge of the ledger has been beveled so that it's flush with the underside of the carriages. Before nailing the carriages, make sure that they fit snugly against both the stairwell header and the underside of the subfloor. Once everything is tacked down, check the rise cuts for plumb and the run cuts for level, then use a long level to make sure the carriage cuts are all in the same plane.

Under-stair framing. The upper and lower carriages define the space underneath the stairs. Regardless of whether the space is closed off or made into a closet, the drywall will lap up over the carriages. However, because the carriages will be covered with an oak skirtboard, the drywall doesn't have to be trimmed to the sawtooth pattern of the carriages. It can be stopped a little short of the rise and run cuts, since the skirt will cover any gaps.

Frame the under-stair area as if it were a conventional wall, with studs on 16-in. centers, as shown in the photo on the facing page. Note that I've nailed a 2x4 flatwise on the bottom of the carriages to give the tops of the studs extra purchase. A closet or bathroom door will need a header, of course, as well as king studs and trimmers.

The housed stringer

Now that the cut carriages are in place, it's time to build the housed stringer, a job that's a bit more involved. As I mentioned earlier in the chapter, the closed-side risers and treads fit into tapered mortises routed in the housed stringer and are locked in place by glued wedges. In addition, the treads are joined to the risers by housed dado and tongue-and-groove joints, as shown in the photos at right and below.

Although it looks complicated, it's not that difficult to make the housed stringer. It does require careful layout, but the mortises themselves will be cut with a jig-guided router. The grooves and dadoes in the treads and risers can be cut with a router or on the table saw. For this stair, the housed stringer is attached directly to the wall studs after the drywall, but it could just as easily be installed before drywalling, providing it were held away from the wall with spacers. The drywall could then be butted directly to the edge of the stringer and covered with trim.

Because they have to accept mortises, the housed stringers are a full 1¼-in. thick oak (milled from 5/4 rough stock), 10½ in. wide and as long as the cut carriages. Make sure that the stringer has straight, parallel edges and isn't warped or twisted. The treads, by the way, are factory-made, but I made my own risers from oak planks. The treads are 1⅛ in. thick by 12 in. wide, the risers ¾ in. thick by 9 in. high. These are rough overall sizes that will be trimmed to final size at assembly.

The understair framing (facing page) can enclose a closet, a bathroom or another stairwell to the basement. A 2x4 nailed flatwise to the upper carriage gives studs better nailing purchase. On the stair's wall side, the treads and risers fit into mortises routed in the housed stringer (above right). Wedges driven into the mortises lock the parts in place (right).

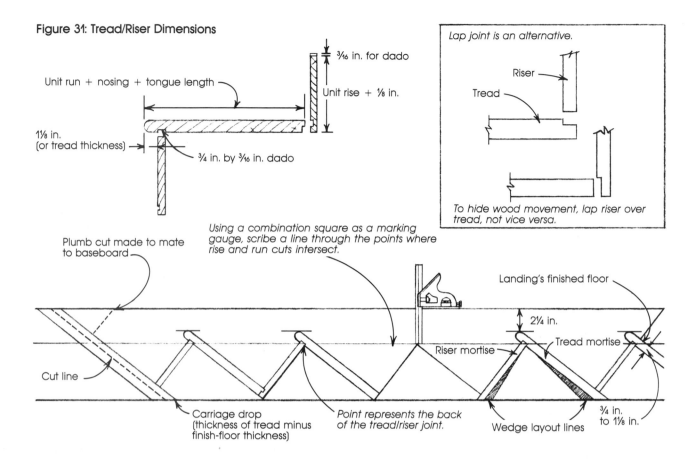

Figure 31: Tread/Riser Dimensions

Lap joint is an alternative.

Riser

Tread

To hide wood movement, lap riser over tread, not vice versa.

¾6 in. for dado

Unit rise + ⅛ in.

Unit run + nosing + tongue length

1⅛ in. (or tread thickness)

¾ in. by ¾6 in. dado

Plumb cut made to mate to baseboard

Using a combination square as a marking gauge, scribe a line through the points where rise and run cuts intersect.

Landing's finished floor

2¼ in.

Tread mortise

Riser mortise

Cut line

Carriage drop (thickness of tread minus finish-floor thickness)

Point represents the back of the tread/riser joint.

Wedge layout lines

¾ in. to 1⅛ in.

Housed-stringer layout. Although housed stringers and cut carriages have the same rise and run, laying out a housed stringer is a little different from laying out a cut carriage. As you can see in the bottom photo on p. 67, the treads and risers stop short of the top edge of the housed stringer, rather than sitting on top of the carriage, as they do on the cut carriage side. For this stair, the housed stringer stands 2¼ in. proud of the tread nosing.

To begin layout, first cut off a 1-in. slice of the actual tread material you'll be using. On this piece, mark the nosing and the dado for the riser, as shown in Figure 31. Set the marked piece on the stringer stock (it doesn't matter where at this point) and position it so that it's at the same angle as the run cuts on the cut carriage. If need be, use your square and lightly pencil in a rise/run layout. Next, slide the piece until the nosing is 2¼ in. from the edge of the skirtboard.

You can now mark the point where the back of the riser intersects the underside of the tread. Using a combination square as a marking gauge, scribe a line through this point that's the length of the stringer board and parallel to its top edge, as shown in Figure 31. The sawtooth point of the rise/run layout will just touch this line, and if everything works out correctly, the sawtooth points on the cut carriages will eventually be in the identical plane.

Use your framing square to mark in the rise and run cuts, as shown in Figure 31. (Also use the Pythagorean theorem to check the layout's total length.) These lines represent the undersides of the treads and risers. Since the treads and risers are housed, the mortises must be marked for cutting. To do this, use a slice of tread as a template and mark the mortise with a sharp pencil, as shown in the photo on the facing page. You'll have to mark for the wedges, too. Figure 32 shows how to make the wedges; you'll need two for each tread/riser pair.

At this point, it's pretty easy to see where the bottom cut on the stringer is made. Since the top surface of the bottommost tread is penciled in, just measure down one unit rise to the finished floor, then add an allowance for the floor material that's not yet in place. Also, draw in the vertical cut line (plumb line) where the baseboard butts to the stringer. This is illustrated in Figure 31.

The top cut is just as simple. The vertical cut line is the same as the layout line for the back side of the top riser. Since the back of the riser is right up against the hanger-board, the vertical face of the housed stringer is too. This doesn't leave room for full-size wedges on this riser, but a very thin wedge inserted between the riser and the hanger-board will force the top riser tight against the show side of the mortise in the housed stringer.

NOSING DETAIL

Rabbet out a section of the tread; groove back edge to mate with the flooring.

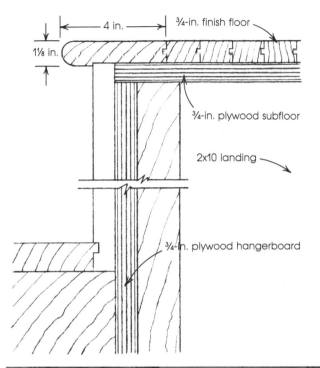

4 in.

¾-in. finish floor

1⅛ in.

¾-in. plywood subfloor

2x10 landing

¾-in. plywood hangerboard

Figure 32: Making the Wedges

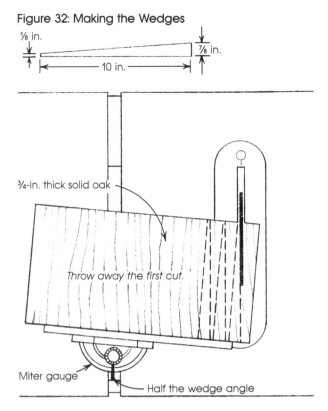

⅛ in.

⅞ in.

10 in.

¾-in. thick solid oak

Throw away the first cut.

Miter gauge

Half the wedge angle

Make the cut, flip the stock edge for edge, then make the next cut.

To mark out the tread, riser and wedge mortises, scribe the rise/run lines and then use the actual parts as templates.

Figure 33: Router Mortising Jigs

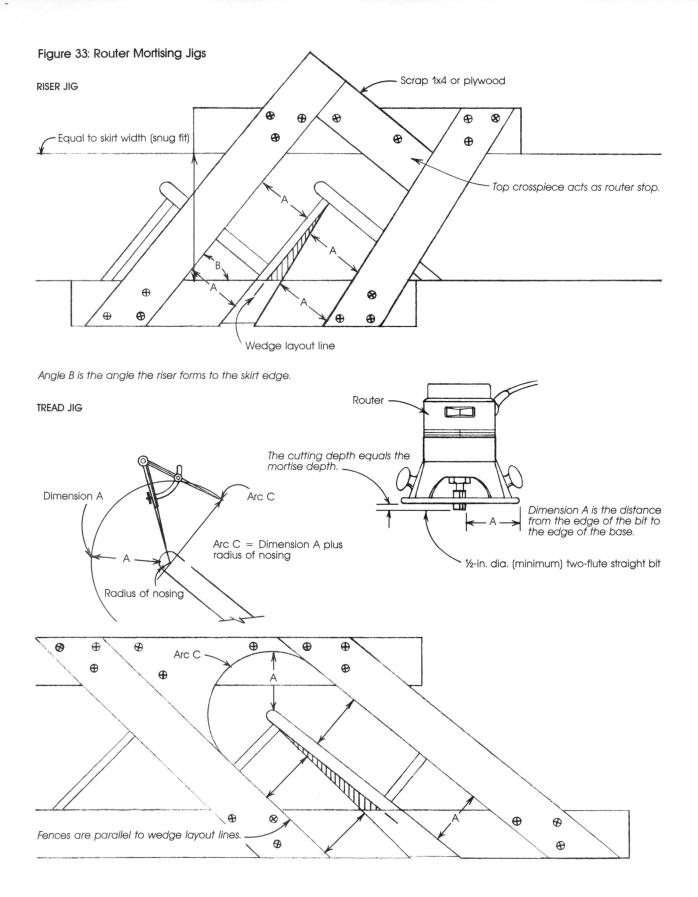

RISER JIG

Scrap 1x4 or plywood

Equal to skirt width (snug fit)

Top crosspiece acts as router stop.

A

A

B

A

A

Wedge layout line

Angle B is the angle the riser forms to the skirt edge.

TREAD JIG

Router

The cutting depth equals the mortise depth.

Dimension A

Arc C

Arc C = Dimension A plus radius of nosing

A

Radius of nosing

Dimension A is the distance from the edge of the bit to the edge of the base.

A

½-in. dia. (minimum) two-flute straight bit

Arc C

A

A

A

Fences are parallel to wedge layout lines.

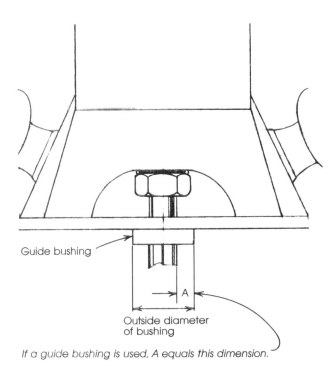

Guide bushing

A

Outside diameter
of bushing

If a guide bushing is used, A equals this dimension.

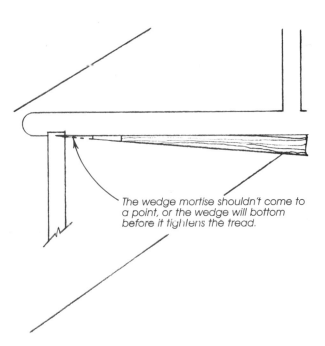

The wedge mortise shouldn't come to a point, or the wedge will bottom before it tightens the tread.

Actually, this top riser can butt right into the stringer instead of being housed, because it's well supported by the hangerboard. The nosing on the landing will also butt into the stringer, since it isn't practical to house it in the stringer. In the videotape, I didn't rout mortises for all the treads and risers, so I could explain that it's quite practical to butt treads and risers, as long as they are supported by cut carriages.

Double-check your layout, then saw the top and bottom housed-stringer cuts. Position the stringer in place temporarily; then put an actual tread in place, resting it on the two cut carriages installed earlier. The tread should rest fully on both cut carriages, and the housed-stringer end of the tread should align with the mortise markout lines. Check the risers too. You may find small misalignments, but any greater than 1/16 in. might signal an incorrect layout. Don't forget to check the first and last rises to ensure a consistent unit rise from finish floor to finish floor.

Routing the mortises. The housed-stringer mortises can be chopped by hand with chisels, but it's tedious work that I wouldn't wish on anybody. It's far better to use a router and shopmade jig. Together, these will do the job in a fraction of the time and yield more accurate results. Any router will do, providing it has at least 1 hp and will accept 1/2-in. shank bits. Smaller bits can't handle the high cutting loads. A plunge-type router, like the Makita I have, is convenient but not absolutely necessary.

Two jigs are required, one for the tread mortise and one for the riser. Depending on the kind of router you use, there are three ways to make the jigs. My Makita has a round base, so it's convenient to make a jig that references right to the router's base. Other kinds of routers, such as the older Makita square-based models, have template guide bushings. These are sleeve-like devices through which the bit penetrates, allowing the outside of the sleeve to ride against a template or jig. A third type of jig references against a guide bearing pressed on the shank above the cutter. This type is described in greater detail in Chapter 6. Figure 33 shows the principles for edge-guided and bushing guided routers. For this stair, I built the edge-guided jig.

As shown in the photos on p. 72, the jigs are simply fences that guide the router cut. The chief trick in building them is to ensure that the fences are positioned away from the layout lines by a dimension exactly equal to the distance between the bit's cutting radius and the edge of the router base. Instead of measuring this dimension on the router and transferring it to the wood, I find it more accurate simply to lower the router bit over the area to be cut until it just touches the work. Unplug the router and spin the bit by hand so that its cutting arc is tangent to the layout line, then mark the edge of the router's base directly on the board. Do this at each end of the mortise, then connect the points with a straightedge. Don't forget to allow for the wedges. Also make sure that the bit is

Router mortising jigs for the treads and risers can be made in place by clamping scrap 1x4 or plywood fences at the correct distances from the layout lines, then screwing them together. Clamp the jigs to the stringer, then rout carefully, always feeding the router from left to right.

concentric to the router base; if it's not, always reference the same point on the router base to the jig.

So much for the straight cuts. Allowing for the tread nosing is more difficult. You can't simply expand the layout lines as you did with the straight cuts. One solution is to bore a blind hole with a bit whose radius matches the nosing diameter. This assumes, however, that the nosing is a semicircle rather than a segment of an arc (which it usually is). The practical solution is to find the approximate radius of the tread nosing arc and, with a large compass set to the appropriate radius, scribe the larger arc on the jig, as shown in Figure 33 on p. 70. Note that the arc of the nosing forms a corner with both straight sides of the treads. The router bit can't make this corner, so it will require touchup with a chisel.

Before laying out the nosing arc, check the treads for accurate factory nosings. They're often irregular, making for a poor fit in the precisely milled mortise. It's a wise idea to standardize the nosing shape by routing the edges yourself with a large-diameter roundover bit.

With the layout lines of the mortises enlarged, you can now build the jig. I use 1x3 or 1x4 pine or plywood scraps for fences and plywood or hardboard for the nosing template. When cutting the jig parts, make sure the taper for the tread wedge doesn't come all the way out to the nosing. Keep it behind the riser so there won't be a gap on the exposed side. This may require a little fussing with the jig to create a small step in the mortise. The small step also gives the wedge a little breathing room, so it won't bottom out in the mortise before it's driven home.

Screw the parts together so they can't flex. The riser jig is made in the same way, but it's a lot easier to make because there's no radiused nosing. Rout a scrap piece to fine-tune the jigs and check the fit with tread, riser and wedges. Don't get exasperated if the nosing doesn't fit exactly. Small cracks can be taken up when each tread is fitted. If the jigs check out, go ahead and rout the mortises (see the photo on p. 73). Clamp the jigs firmly, and to keep the router from grabbing the wood and ruining the cut, feed from left to right, or clockwise around the arc.

Clean up any rough spots with a chisel, then hang both the upper and the lower skirt by screwing them to the wall. Place as many screws as you can behind or below the mortises, as shown in the photo below. If you can't avoid exposed screws, plan to countersink the screw holes and hide them with wooden plugs.

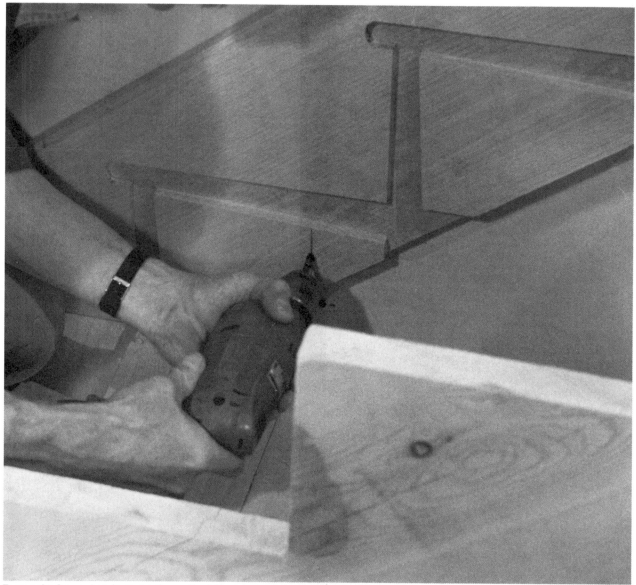

Fasten the housed stringer to the wall with screws driven just below the mortises, where they will be hidden by the treads and risers.

Treads and risers

For the straight stair described in Chapter 3, the treads and risers are simply nailed to the cut carriages. This works fine, because the plywood treads and risers are covered by carpet. An oak stair, though, is something special. To give it a refined look, the risers are mitered into a skirt fastened to the open-side carriage. This mitered skirt is not a structural member, however. The cut carriage supports the tread.

The mitered skirt is made from ¾-in. thick oak that's a little wider than the closed skirt so it will lap well over the drywall. I make it from a straight, flat oak board at least 11 in. wide. To begin the layout, scribe a line 1 in. back from the upper edge of the skirt, as shown in Figure 34. Reset the buttons, then draw in the tread/riser cuts so they intersect this setback line.

There is one quirk in laying out the mitered skirt. In a regular cut carriage, the horizontal cuts represent the bottoms of the treads, the vertical cuts the back of the risers. In this case, we still want the horizontal cut to be the bottom of the tread but the vertical line must represent the front of the riser. Remember that we'll be mitering back from this line. Therefore, we add the thickness of a riser to the riser layout lines. This will be the toe of the miter, while the original line is the heel.

Figure 34: Mitered-Skirt Layout

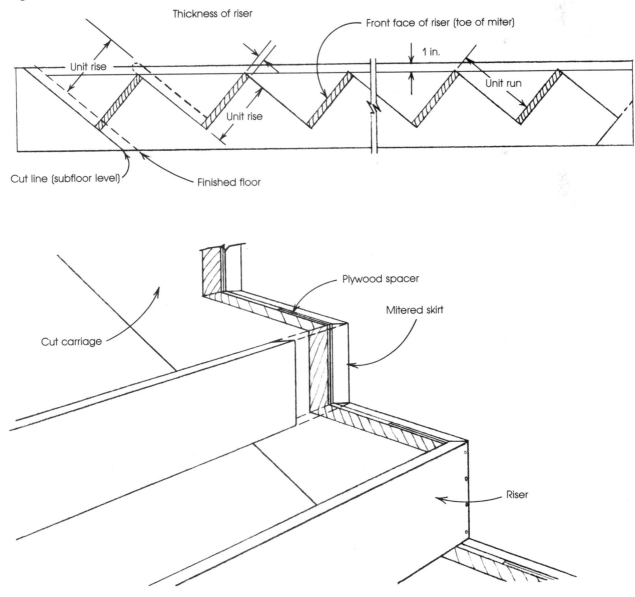

Saw the tread and riser cuts on the mitered skirt with a circular saw (facing page). Then mark out the miters with a bevel gauge (above) and saw them with a handsaw (right).

The bottom cut is figured in the usual way, but it's hard to predict the top cut precisely at this point. The vertical cut will be housed by a notch in the newel post. This notch allows some latitude, but I suggest waiting until "post time" to make the cut. For now, extend it almost into the inside corner formed by the upper and lower stair. The upper-flight skirt will also be housed in a notch in the landing newel later on. It may be necessary to install the landing newel temporarily before the upper-flight mitered skirt can be installed.

Saw the mitered skirt with a circular saw, as shown in the photo on the facing page. Cut right to the line on the tread and don't worry about slight imperfections; they will be

covered later by molding. But stay well away from the layout line for the miter. It will be cut with a handsaw next.

Mitering with a handsaw requires a lot of concentration, but it's easier if you clamp the work at waist height. I clamp one end to a wall and the other to a sawhorse. Lay out the 45° miter and saw it with a fine-tooth (12 tooth-per-inch) handsaw. The trick is to cut the miter slightly more acute than required, so the toe will fit tightly with a bit of open space at the heel (which won't be seen). Lower the skirt when necessary to make cutting comfortable.

The mitered skirt is attached to the outer cut carriages, but in between there's ½ in. of drywall and ¼ in. of extra space. The extra space allows us to move the skirt in and

Spacers tacked between the cut carriage and mitered skirt allow the skirt to be repositioned slightly when you are fitting the risers.

out to fine-tune the riser miters. To create this gap, I tack scraps of ¾-in. plywood to the cut carriage. At the bottom, I nail and glue on a full plywood piece, with no drywall. The bottom newel will be bolted in this area, and I want all the thread purchase I can get.

Clamp the skirt in its finished position after making the bottom and top cuts. Don't nail yet—that will be done when the risers are installed. With the skirt clamped in place, check that all cuts are plumb and level and try a riser for fit. The back should sit tight against the cut carriages, while the front face should line up with the miter of the skirt and the mortise of the housed stringer. Make sure the mitered skirt's tread cuts are even or just below the tread cuts of the cut carriage. The mitered skirt is not intended to support any weight at all. Any small gaps between the tread and mitered skirt will be covered with cove molding later. Don't forget to sand these two skirts before they're tacked in place.

Tread talk. Tread stock is commonly available in standard lengths of 3 ft., 3 ft. 6 in. and 4 ft., and less commonly in 5-ft., 6-ft. and 8-ft. lengths. It is usually a full 1⅛ in. thick, and I wouldn't recommend using anything less. Widths are usually 11½ in. Oak and fir are the two most popular species for stair treads. Fir is usually vertical grain rather than flat grain. Vertical grain is more wear resistant and dimensionally stable and has a subtle, striated figure.

If you're really particular, you can find oak tread stock that's made of a single board, but try to find quartersawn boards. Wide plainsawn stock will warp. More than likely, though, treads will be laminated of several narrower boards. If the grain hasn't been matched carefully—which it usually isn't—the stair will have a rather garish, zebra-stripe look.

For this stair, the unit run is 10 in. To this figure we need to add 1⅛ in. for the nosing and another ¼ in. at the back for the tongue, which fits into a groove in the riser. This adds up to a total width of 11⅜ in. The tread length will be 36 in. from the finished face of the housed stringer to the centerline of the balustrade, which is also the centerline of the mitered skirt. To this add ½ in. for the mortise, another ⅜ in. to reach the outside of the mitered skirt and another 1⅛ in. for the return nosing, for a total minimum length of 38 in. Leave the treads several inches longer than that for now. Although the return nosing will be stuck onto the end of the tread, there is still a "horn" on the front edge of the tread that is mitered to this nosing.

The risers are cut from ¾-in. thick oak. They're 7¹¹⁄₁₆ in. wide (the unit rise) plus ³⁄₁₆ in. for the dado in the bottom of the tread, for a total width of 7⅞ in. The length of the risers is 36 in. plus ½ in. for the mortise plus another ⅜ in. to get past the centerline of the balustrade. This totals 36⅞ in. In the best work, the tread and riser are joined by a tongue and groove.

Load on the treads should be carried by the carriages, not the mitered skirt. With the skirt in place, check to see that its top edge is slightly below the carriage's tread cut.

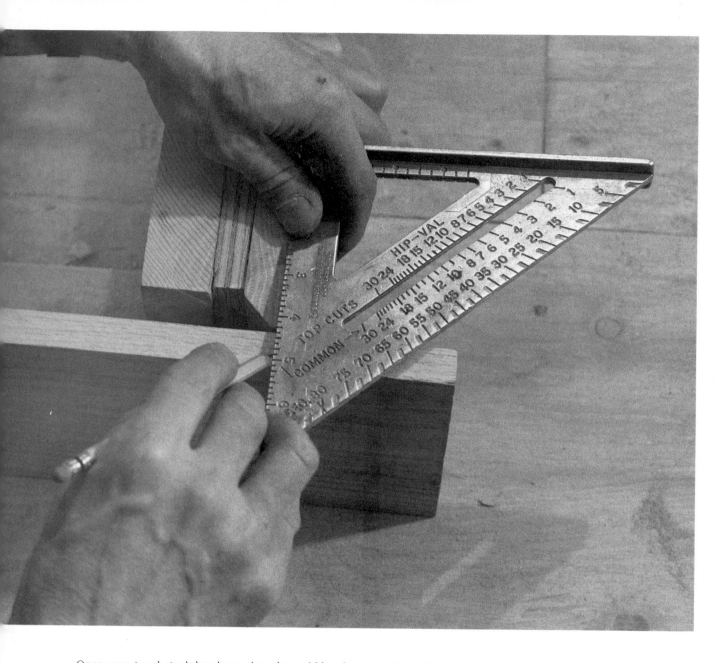

Once your tread stock has been ripped to width, plow dadoes in the bottom of each tread for the riser and cut the tongue at the back of the tread. These operations can be accomplished with a router or a dado head on the table saw. The dado for the riser in the bottom of each tread should be about ³⁄₁₆ in. deep. If it's any deeper it will weaken the nosing, and if it's too shallow it won't provide enough margin for shrinkage. The riser should seat to the bottom of the dado to eliminate any weakness caused by the tread being cantilevered at its thinnest spot. To ensure a tight fit, make the groove in the riser a little deeper than the ¼-in. long tongue, so there's no danger of the tongue bottoming out.

Installing treads and risers. I start with the bottom riser and work my way up. As in the straight stair, the bottom riser is a tread thickness narrower than the rest, since its bottom edge butts the floor instead of joining to a tread. To mark the riser's length for cutting, hold it in place and use a square to mark the toe of the miter, as shown in the photo above. Make sure the riser is bottomed out in the mortise of the closed skirt. Saw the miter on a table saw if you have one or by hand, back-cutting it slightly if necessary to ensure a tight fit.

Check the miter for fit. If it's open at the toe but tight at the heel, trim the miter with a hand plane, a handsaw or on the table saw until it fits. Take your time and make

Mark out the riser miters directly from the mitered skirt (facing page), saw them on a table saw or radial-arm saw, and check the fit. In the photo above left, the miter has been back cut slightly, producing a tight fit at the miter's toe. The tongue of the bottom tread is nipped off to clear the mitered skirt (above right).

very shallow cuts; otherwise you risk making the piece too short. Once the riser does fit, apply a thin bead of adhesive to both pieces and drive 6d finish nails through predrilled holes. Nail the miter from both directions. Apply adhesive between the riser and the carriages as well, then face-nail these. You can use carpenter's yellow or white glue when the joints are tight, but construction adhesive is a better gap filler. On the closed-skirt side, you'll have to do some fiddling to get the wedge in. Because you can't drive the wedge in from below, as you will with the other risers, it may take some levering with a crowbar to force it in. Spread a little yellow glue in both the mortise and on the wedge.

Mitered returns on the treads. Trim the second riser and tack it in place temporarily, and you're ready to fit the first tread. As mentioned earlier, each tread has a mitered return to hide the end grain. The return consists of a small cross-grain piece glued onto the end grain, and the mitering should be done before the tread is cut to length and installed. The lowermost tread, the landing treads and the uppermost tread get treated a little differently. I'll cover that later.

I saw the miter return on the table saw, then finish it with a handsaw, as shown in the photo above. It is easier to cut this miter by hand if you've left the tread a little overlong. That way, you can start the miter cut on the front edge of the tread rather than right at the corner. When sawing the straight cut on the table saw, you won't be able to see the underside of the cut, so stop the cut well short of the miter and finish it up with the handsaw. The actual returns can be glued on once the newel posts are installed.

Once the return is cut, check the tread for fit. Right at the outset, you'll find that the outermost corner of the tongue on the back of the tread will need to be nipped off at a 45° angle to clear the mitered skirt. The lower riser should seat in its dado. Tap a wedge gently in place to pull the tread up tight in the mortise. The miter return cut should be flush with the outside face of the mitered skirt,

Before the treads are installed, saw the return miter with a table saw and a handsaw. Later, the nosing will be returned with short sections of nosing.

while the horn that forms the actual return should stand proud by an amount equal to the tread thickness. If the cut isn't flush, you should be able to move the tread in or out a bit until it is. Remember that adjustments can still be made by trimming the tread at the mortise end.

See that the nosing fits into its mortise. It may be hard to slide the tread forward because it's locked to the riser beneath it. To adjust the fit, you'll have to widen the dado a little or plane a bit off the back of the riser. Any gaps in the dado will be underneath the tread and will, in any case, be hidden by cove molding. Watch for riser height problems as well. If the riser is too tall, the tread won't seat on the carriages. If it's too short, the riser won't seat

in the dado and you'll have to shim it or, in extreme cases, make a new riser.

Similarly, gaps between the carriages and the treads or risers can be taken up with thin shims. A carriage that's consistently too low or high at either end should be corrected with a single adjustment (a wedge between the carriage and the floor) rather than adjusting each step. High spots in the carriages that force treads and risers out of plane with the housed-stringer mortises should be trimmed with a chisel. Make sure everything is plumb and level in all directions. Use a square to check the angle between tread and riser. If you have a problem with the first tread and riser, make sure it's not happening with the rest too.

Smear each wedge with glue, then tap it in from behind. Check the front of the riser for a tight fit in the mortise.

Fastening treads and risers. Once you're satisfied with the fit, bore pilot holes for screws through the back of the riser into its mating tread. Then remove both tread and riser, apply yellow glue to the tongue-and-groove joint and assemble the riser and tread loosely with screws in the holes you just bored. Apply a thin bead of construction adhesive to the top of the bottom riser and also to the miter between the riser and skirt. Wiggle this assembly into place, then nail the miter. Smear liberal amounts of glue on the underside of the mortise and on the wedges, then tap them home.

Finish screwing the riser to the tread, then fix the tread to the cut carriages with finish nails or screws. If you're nailing, use 12d finish nails in predrilled holes for the treads and 6d for the risers. I prefer to screw the treads, as they're less likely to work loose and squeak. The screw holes can be plugged with wooden bungs. I don't use screws for the risers, though, as all those bungs look like too many polka dots. Since the mitered skirt isn't structural, the treads needn't be attached to it, just the risers. Do screw the tread to the outer carriage, however, and don't forget to use construction adhesive between both treads and risers and the carriages.

Where the treads meet the cut carriages or behind the tread/riser joints, glue blocks add strength and reduce squeaks. These should be bedded in plenty of glue and screwed too, as shown in the top right photo on the facing page.

In the photos and videotape, you'll notice that I'm using drywall screws. That's because these screws have self-starting points and deep threads so they don't require pilot holes in soft materials (although you'll need pilot holes for hardwoods). These screws are very brittle and will snap off if abused. If the screw is howling in protest as you drive it home, stop and drill a larger or deeper pilot hole. A little soap or wax on the screw threads helps.

In addition to the glued wedges, the treads are screwed into the carriages and the risers are screwed into the back of the treads. Glue blocks at the riser/tread intersection reduce squeaks.

The nosing returns are glued and nailed to the end of the treads, as shown at left. The back end of the nosing is also returned with a small mitered block, as shown below. In the photo on the facing page, Schuttner has nearly completed the lower flight. Mitered returns have been installed on the treads here, but normally this job is done after the newels are installed.

This completes one step. The rest follow in a similar way. In the top left photo on p. 85, you can see that the bottom tread is flush with the mitered skirt: it has no return. The return will be pieced in around the bottom newel post later. (The photos on the facing page show return-mitered treads.) To complete the lower flight, just continue the process described above. Once the treads and risers of the lower flight are in place, plan to install the starting newel and the landing newel. Traditionally, skirts, treads and risers were mortised into the landing newel, making it a bit of a jigsaw puzzle to assemble. Its geometry makes it impossible to install if both flights are in place, so refer to Chapter 5 to see how the newels are made and installed. Once they're fastened, you can move on to the upper flight, whose treads and risers are installed just as the lower ones were.

Instead of wedged mortises, you can simply butt the tread and risers to the skirtboard, as shown. However, wood movement may open gaps between the treads and skirt. Minor misfits between the carriage and riser can be closed with wedges.

A few shortcuts

Thus far, I've described top-of-the-line stair construction, which is fine if you have the skill, the time and the patience. But there are some ways to simplify the process that won't appreciably change the look or the quality of the finished job.

Instead of a housed stringer, the treads and risers can simply butt into a plain skirt, in which case you'll have to install a third cut carriage, as described in Chapter 3. This carriage will be exactly the same as the other two. It can be installed with a spacer to allow the skirt to be inserted later, or the skirt can be installed first, then the carriage held tight to it. In either case, the skirt should be thinner, since it won't have mortises.

The main problem with butt joints is that, over time, a gap may open between the skirt and treads. It may help to use adhesive on the ends of the butt joints or somehow to screw the joint through the backside of the skirt and into the butt ends of the treads and risers. This would have to be done by pre-assembling the flight, which is probably as much work or more than making the mortises.

Similarly, you can eliminate the tongue-and-groove joint that joins the back of the treads to the risers. A simple butt joint, glued and screwed, or a lap joint will work too. If you choose a lap, however, be sure to lap the riser over the tread instead of the tread over the riser. As shown in Figure 31 on p. 68, a tread-over-riser joint will show gaps caused by wood movement.

The mitered skirt is harder to avoid, but it's possible to have the ends of the risers stand proud of the face of the outer skirt. This shows end grain, of course, but some sort of decorative shaping might make it less objectionable. Similarly, the treads don't have to be return-mitered. They can be shaped instead. One other alternative to the mitered skirt is brackets, which are individual pieces mitered to the ends of the risers and fastened to the carriage, as shown in Figure 35.

Figure 35: Alternative Tread Designs

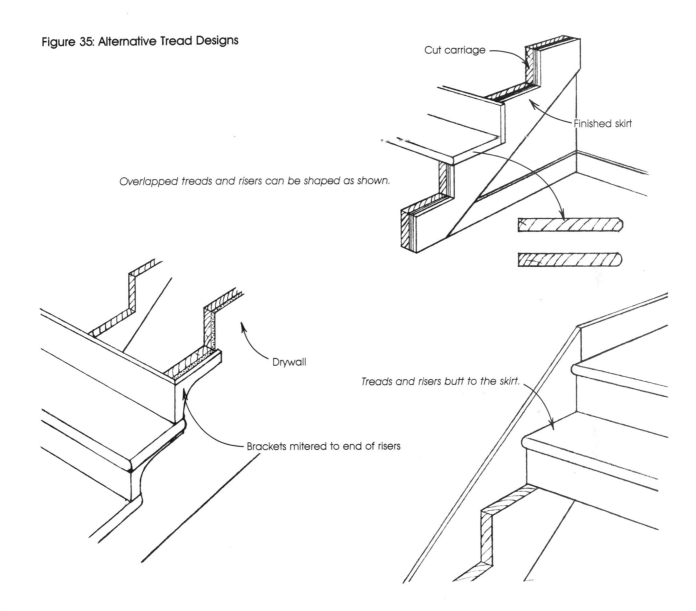

Cut carriage

Finished skirt

Overlapped treads and risers can be shaped as shown.

Drywall

Brackets mitered to end of risers

Treads and risers butt to the skirt.

Schuttner's L-shaped stair has a simple balustrade consisting of chamfered oak newels and balusters.

An L-Shaped Stair: Newels, Rails and Balusters

Chapter 5

We negotiate a stair by climbing the treads and risers, but it is the balustrade—the newels, the balusters and the handrail—that gives an open stair its finished look. And, of course, the balustrade is an essential safety device on an open stair, even on one that has a rail attached to the closed side.

There are two kinds of balustrades: post-to-post systems in which the rail is fitted between newel posts, and over-the-post designs, in which the rail is mounted on top of the newel posts. With its carved volutes, easements and goosenecks, over-the-post railing is a craft unto itself, so I'll limit my discussion here to post-to-post design with site-made newels of square section. You can buy factory-made stair parts for balustrades, but I find it more satisfying to make my own.

Newels are the real structural beef of the balustrade. Because people tend to swing their weight around the newels, anchoring them securely is the key to a durable, rock-solid balustrade. My balustrade construction method is by no means the only one, nor is it necessarily the best; my balustrade design represents a practical compromise between strength and economy of construction.

Newel design

The stair that I built for this book and videotape has three newels, one at the bottom (called the starting newel), one at the landing and one at the top. The newel at the landing, called an angle newel, is the longest because it has to accept railings intersecting in two planes. The top newel, which changes the railing from sloped to horizontal, is called the landing newel.

In very elaborate work, newels were traditionally hollow, box-like structures with solid wood caps. Hollow newel posts can be built with an internal steel tensioning rod that passes through a metal plate near the top of the newel. This rod extends beneath the floor through another metal plate, and the post is slipped over the rod and a nut tightened from the top. It's very involved construction that's beyond the scope of this book.

My newel posts are solid oak, made from two pieces laminated together from the same board to minimize twisting. Because the pieces are matched on the glue line side, the joint is invisible. The posts are nominally 4x4, finishing out to 3¾ in. square. You can vary this size to suit your stair. Just make sure that the post is big enough to stand proud of any tread nosings that butt against it. As a rough length, 4 ft. is long enough for the starting newel (add a foot if it's to go through the floor) and 5 ft. is plenty for the angle and landing newels.

For decoration, I've stop-chamfered all four edges of each newel with a router and beveled the tops with my chopsaw, as shown in Figure 36 on p. 92. Other decorative treatments are possible, but don't add them until after you fit the posts, or they might interfere with the joinery. It's also nice to have square corners for laying out the posts.

Newel layout. As discussed in Chapter 4, the centerline of the balustrade and of all its various elements is located in the center of the mitered skirt's thickness, as shown in Figure 36 on p. 92. By using this centerline as a datum, parts of varying thickness can be made to align correctly. This is particularly helpful for laying out the notches that allow the newels to fit around the mitered skirt and around the treads.

Figure 36: Newel-Post Layout

Posts are glued up from two pieces of the same board; 4 ft. to 5 ft. is typical newel length.

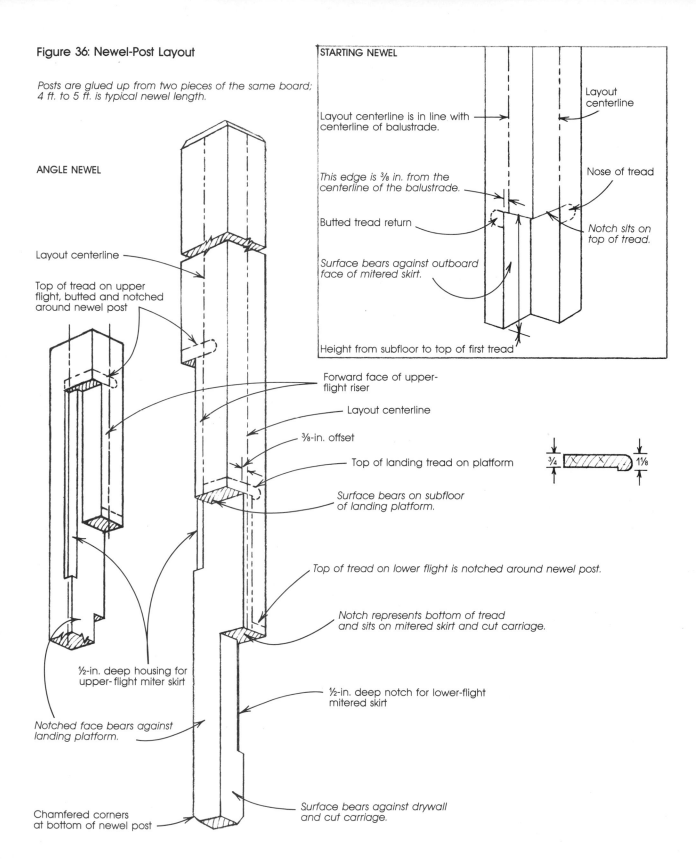

ANGLE NEWEL

Layout centerline

Top of tread on upper flight, butted and notched around newel post

Forward face of upper-flight riser

Layout centerline

³⁄₈-in. offset

Top of landing tread on platform

Surface bears on subfloor of landing platform.

Top of tread on lower flight is notched around newel post.

Notch represents bottom of tread and sits on mitered skirt and cut carriage.

½-in. deep housing for upper-flight miter skirt

½-in. deep notch for lower-flight mitered skirt

Notched face bears against landing platform.

Chamfered corners at bottom of newel post

Surface bears against drywall and cut carriage.

STARTING NEWEL

Layout centerline is in line with centerline of balustrade.

Layout centerline

This edge is ³⁄₈ in. from the centerline of the balustrade.

Nose of tread

Butted tread return

Notch sits on top of tread.

Surface bears against outboard face of mitered skirt.

Height from subfloor to top of first tread

¾   1⅛

The newels are chamfered with a router, but only after notches for the steps have been laid out and cut. The notches are laid out from the balustrade center-line, as shown in the photo above right.

Both the starting newel and the angle newel are notched to fit around the treads, risers and skirt. Once notched, they're both bolted in place with lag screws.

As shown in Figure 36 on p. 92, the starting newel has a relatively simple notch, the angle newel a more complex one that fits around both the lower and the upper mitered skirts. Laying out and cutting the starting-newel notch is straightforward. Refer to Figure 36 for specific dimensions, although these will vary somewhat from stair to stair. Also, if the post is going to penetrate the floor to fasten to the floor framing, adjust the notch to allow for it. The notch is hogged out with a circular saw and router, then finished up with careful chisel cuts. Later, I'll trim the notch further when I plumb the post at installation. Note in the photo at left on the facing page that the tread also has a notch, which I cut with a handsaw.

The notches for the angle newel are far more complicated and are best seen in Figure 36. The drawing gives a good general idea of the shape and location of the notches. Again, dimensions will vary slightly with each stair. The best way to lay out the angle newel is to clamp it in place at the correct height and scribe the necessary marks directly from the stairs, rather than trying to calculate the layout mathematically. Note that the notches overlap each other in length, so be very careful with the layout and cutting. Also note that the centerlines must be carefully positioned because the depth of one mortise affects the width of the other, and vice versa.

Fastening the newels. When possible, I like to pass the starting newel right through the subfloor and fasten it to the floor framing. This vastly increases strength and is always worth the extra effort. If the stair is built before the drywall is up, blocking to support the newel can be nailed or bolted to the joists. A joist that hits in approximately the right spot may be all that's required. The blocking doesn't have to align perfectly as the newel can be shimmed or trimmed, and all of this will be hidden later. Attach a single block perpendicular to the joists or two blocks with a space between big enough for the newel, as shown in Figure 37. Use bolts, not nails, to fasten the newel to the blocking.

If you can't get at the joists from below, judiciously remove sections of the subfloor from above, slip in the necessary blocking, and then piece in the flooring when the newel is done. Sometimes, it's just not practical to anchor the newel to the framing. But at the very least, let the bottom of the starting newel into a mortise chopped in the subflooring or plan to lock it in place by piecing the hardwood flooring around the newel's base.

I lag-bolted the starting newel to the carriage. The lags are angled slightly to the face of the newel so they'll catch the meat of the rough carriage, and they are cross-bolted through the front riser as well. This configuration adds

Figure 37: Newel Attachment Methods

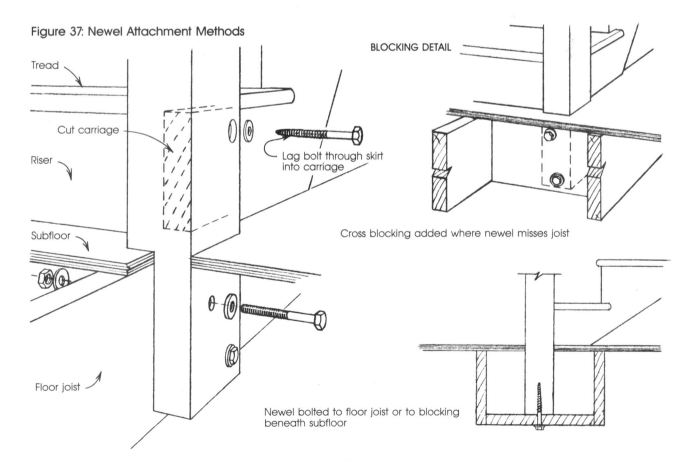

Tread

Cut carriage

Riser

Subfloor

Floor joist

Lag bolt through skirt into carriage

BLOCKING DETAIL

Cross blocking added where newel misses joist

Newel bolted to floor joist or to blocking beneath subfloor

Check with a level to see that both the starting newel and the angle newel are plumb in both planes. The counterbored lag-bolt hole will be plugged with an oak plug.

sturdiness. Each bolt hole is counterbored for a 1-in. dia. wooden plug. Other bolt options include a lag from below the floor into the end grain of the post or from inside the carriage assembly. This eliminates plug holes but requires very precise alignment of the bolt holes and fastening of the newel before the second tread is installed (unless you happen to have some other access to the back of the carriage).

The two upper newels are also bolted. The angle newel is lag-bolted from the back through to the landing fram-

ing; the landing newel is bolted to the carriage. Lagging from the back minimizes plugging of holes without limiting access to these bolts for future tightening. All these newels will probably need some fussing to get them plumb and fitting tightly. It may take trial and error with careful shaving of the mortises to get the post fitting right when the bolts are snug. As the wood expands and contracts with seasonal moisture changes, the posts will loosen, so expect to do some maintenance on newels from time to time.

Installing the balustrade

There are many shapes and sizes for stair handrails, a few of which are shown in Figure 38 below and in Figure 27 on p. 55. In my work, I prefer the shopmade rail shaped from a blank of two 1-in. oak boards laminated together, which is also shown in Figure 38. If these are from the same board, the joint will be unnoticeable. To make the profile pleasant to grasp, I used my router to round the edges and cut coves in the sides. The balusters are let into a $5/16$-in. deep dado cut in the bottom of the rail.

If you make your own railing, glue up the blank and let the glue cure for several days before beginning to shape the rail. If you use factory-made railing, buy enough to span the distance between the posts, plus a little extra for layout and fitting.

The railing fits between the newel posts with angled butt joints. The angle is easily obtained by setting a sliding bevel to the angle formed by the newel and the slope of the stair. Carefully measure and cut one end, then lay the rail right on the treads to scribe the exact length between the two newels. If they're both plumb, the dimension between the bases of the newels will be the same as the dimension at the rail height, which should be 30 in. to 34 in. above the treads. Cut a bit long, then trim the rail's length to a snug fit.

Figure 38: Handrail Designs

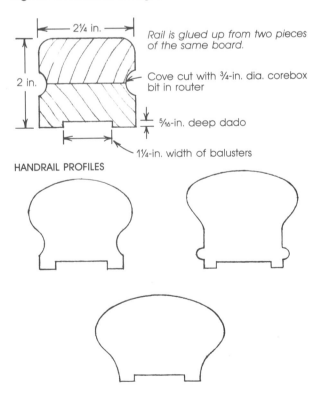

2¼ in.

2 in.

Rail is glued up from two pieces of the same board.

Cove cut with ¾-in. dia. corebox bit in router

5/16-in. deep dado

1¼-in. width of balusters

HANDRAIL PROFILES

The handrail's length and the angle of the butt joint to the newels can be scribed directly from the newel posts, then cut on the chopsaw.

The lower rail is screwed to the starting newel and lag-bolted through the angle newel. The upper rail is handled in the same way.

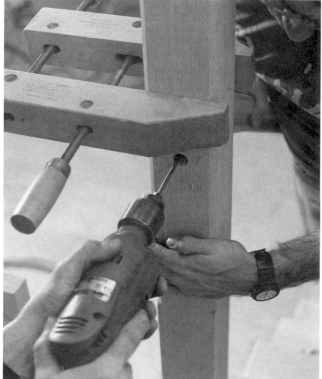

Clamp small blocks or a wood handscrew to the newels to hold the bottom of the rail, then drive 2-in. No. 8 wood or drywall screws from the underside of the rail into the newel, as shown in the top photo on the facing page. The screw heads will be hidden by the filler blocks later. The top end is fastened with a lag bolt driven through the angle newel, the hole later to be covered with a plug.

A rail or hanger bolt is another common way to attach railings to newels or railings to railings. This bolt has wood threads on one end and machine threads on the other. The wood thread end is screwed into the newel. A mating hole is made in the railing. In order to have access to the nut, a large-diameter hole intersecting the smaller bolt hole is bored in the underside of the rail, as shown in Figure 39. The rail is slipped over the machine threads and the nut snugged down. These bolts work fine but can't be used at both ends of a rail without loosening one or two fixed newels. They're best when you don't want plugs on the face of a newel or when you are joining two pieces of railing end-to-end.

The upper railing is installed in the same way, using screws at the lower end and a lag or screws at the top. The height of the railing above the treads is the same as that of the lower rail. The starting point of the upper rail will be about one unit rise higher than the ending of the lower rail and on a perpendicular face of the newel.

Another anchoring method is to let the rail into a mortise chopped in the face of the newel. To lay out the mortise shape, just cut a slice of the railing at the correct angle and trace its outline directly on the newel. Cut the mortise with a router and/or chisels. It may be easier to insert the railing if the railing is relieved on the bottom with a flat cut, as shown in Figure 39. The flat cut won't be visible from the top.

Figure 39: Railing Attachment Methods

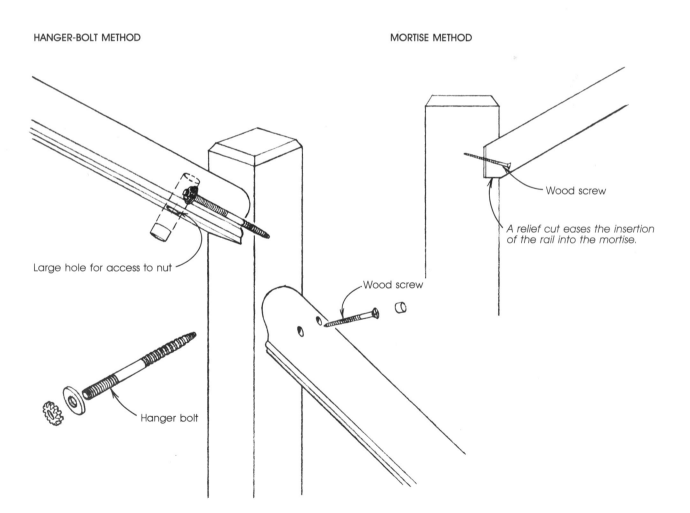

HANGER-BOLT METHOD

MORTISE METHOD

Wood screw

A relief cut eases the insertion of the rail into the mortise.

Large hole for access to nut

Wood screw

Hanger bolt

Figure 40: Baluster Design

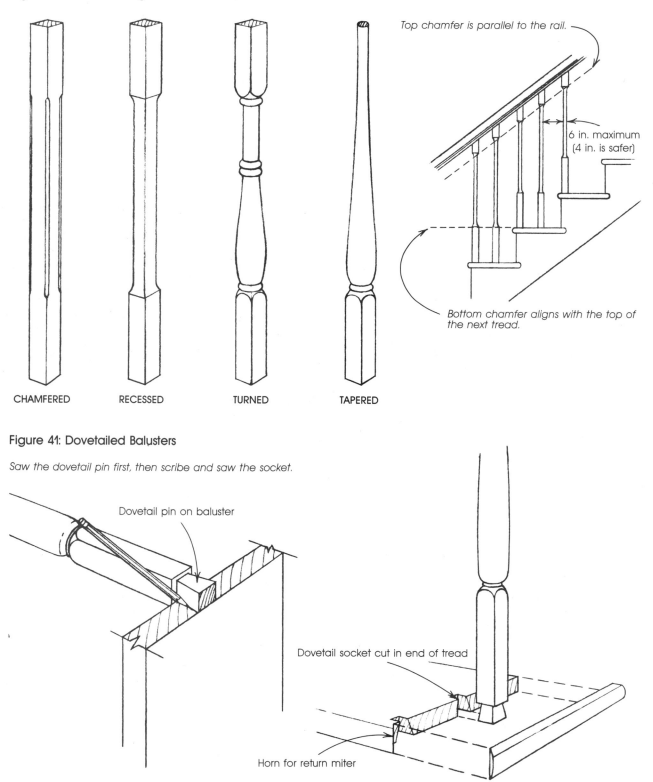

Top chamfer is parallel to the rail.

6 in. maximum
(4 in. is safer)

Bottom chamfer aligns with the top of the next tread.

CHAMFERED   RECESSED   TURNED   TAPERED

Figure 41: Dovetailed Balusters

Saw the dovetail pin first, then scribe and saw the socket.

Dovetail pin on baluster

Dovetail socket cut in end of tread

Horn for return miter

Balusters. As with newels and rails, balusters can be designed in almost infinite variety. Figure 40 shows some of the possibilities. My balusters are 1¼-in. square oak, chamfered to match the newels. At the top, the balusters are housed in the dado in the bottom of the rail and nailed. At the bottom, they're fastened with ½-in. dia. dowels let into holes bored in the treads.

In traditional stair work, the balusters were often dovetailed into the treads and the joints later covered by nailed-on nosing. Dovetailing is a little stronger than doweling but I don't think it's worth the extra effort. If you want to try it, Figure 41 explains the joinery. The dovetails can be cut with the treads in place by using a large dovetail bit in a router. If they are to be sawn by hand and chopped with a chisel, this must be done before the tread is installed. The male portion of the dovetail can be sawn by hand, or a cone can be turned on the end of each baluster and then trimmed square with a chisel.

The balusters are of two different lengths: a short one for the front of each tread and a longer one for midtread, where the railing has ascended another half unit rise. Note that the chamfers on the bottom of both lengths stop even with the top of the next tread, as shown in Figure 40. This is a common alignment reference for the change from square to turned or decorated balusters. However, the chamfers stop parallel with the railing, so the difference in length is made up in the chamfered portion, not in the square sections at the top and bottom.

Baluster spacing is specified by code. Balusters must be close enough to keep a 6-in. dia. ball, representing a child's head, from slipping through. For safety's sake, though, a smaller space is more desirable. With a unit run of 10 in., the balusters for this stair are on 5-in. centers, leaving an open space of 4 in.

Baluster layout should start from the bottom up by first determining where the holes for the dowels will be bored. It's customary for the front face of one baluster on each step to align vertically with the front face of the riser. The mid-tread baluster is centered in the remaining space. Be careful when laying out for the dowel holes. The baluster itself will overlap onto the nosing, but the hole should be well away from the end of the tread.

I measure the length of each baluster in place by positioning the bottom, then using a level to plumb the piece. A mark where the rail crosses the baluster gives me its exact length, as well as the correct angle. To this length, add ⁵⁄₁₆ in. so the baluster will reach the bottom of the handrail's dado. Once it's cut to length, install the baluster with a dab of glue in the dowel hole and nails driven through a predrilled hole at the top of the baluster.

Doweling the end of the balusters is a simple matter of finding the center of the baluster end by drawing diagonals across the corners. Drilling into end grain with a hand drill risks a crooked hole, but it can be done if you're careful and don't drill too deeply. If you want a perfectly straight hole, mount the baluster in a drill press.

Drill the bottom end of the balusters to receive a dowel.

After drilling, mark the balusters' length by scribing directly from the rail (left). Bore the tread's dowel hole (above), install the baluster with a dab of glue on the dowel and nail it at the top through a predrilled hole (facing page).

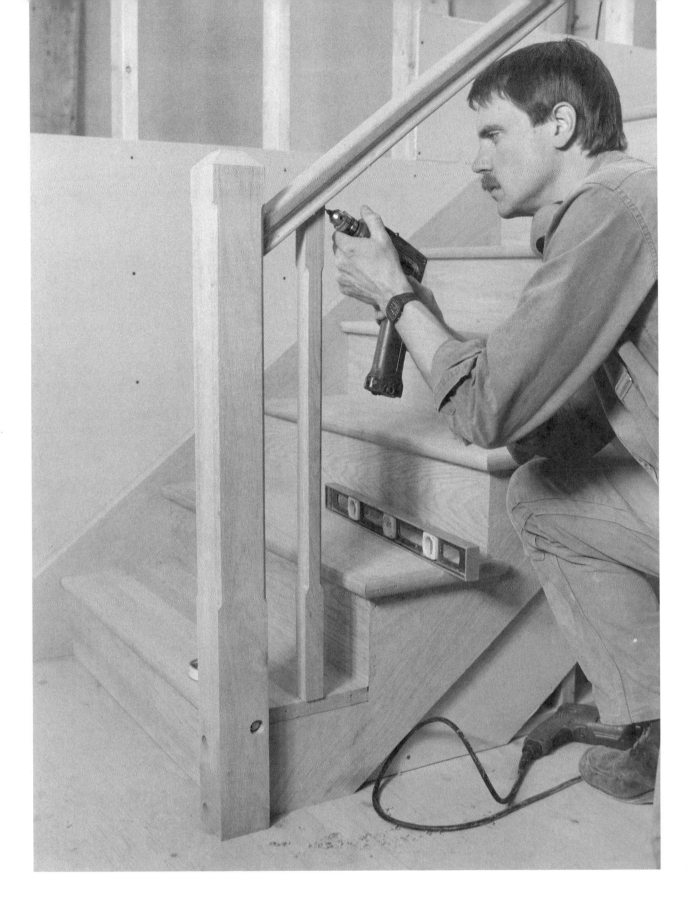

Trimming out the stair. To finish up the stair, the open spaces in the handrail dado between the balusters should be filled in with small blocks, as shown in the photo on the facing page. I make the blocks just a bit thicker than the depth of the dado because it's too hard to get them exactly flush. I mark the blocks in place and cut them, then fasten each one with a couple of small finish nails. Before nailing, chamfer the edges of each spacer with a block plane to produce a nice reveal.

If the nosing hasn't been installed (see Chapter 4), go ahead and install it, then nail on cove molding beneath the treads, as shown in the photo above. Cove molding isn't an absolute necessity, but it dresses up the stair and hides any gaps between the treads and risers. I use ¾-in. cove molding, butted to the housed skirt and mitered at the outside corners. At this point, plugs for any exposed bolt holes should be installed, trimmed flush and prepared for sanding.

Sanding and finishing

Most hardwood stairs will get a varnish finish of some sort, perhaps over stain. It's not uncommon, however, to varnish the treads and paint the risers and skirts. In this case, you may want to delay the application of cove molding or other trim until the painting is done. This will save a lot of tedious cutting in with a brush.

Paint and varnish finishes have the same basic requirements, that is, a smooth surface free of any dirt, stains or surface contamination. As the stair was assembled, each part should have been sanded just before installation. All that remains is to remove any extraneous pencil marks and to do a general cleanup sanding. Set any exposed nails and fill the holes, a process which is an art in itself. Nail holes in the treads ought to be filled with a solvent-based filler, which is harder and will resist wear. Holes not subject to wear can be filled with a softer, oil-based putty. Colored wax fillers also work well, but they're intended to be applied after the finish is on.

Open-pore woods like oak are sometimes filled with an oil-based grain filler to produce a glass-like finish. I don't recommend this, however. Besides being a lot of work, a filler makes for a slick surface, which is the last thing you want on stairs. If you wish, apply a stain after sanding and allow it to dry before varnishing.

The usual choices for a final finish are an alkyd varnish or a polyurethane. Polyurethane is a more durable finish, but I find it to be a little more trouble to apply. It takes longer to set and collects dust while doing so, though the same can be said of alkyd varnish. I personally don't care for the plastic-like look that polyurethane seems to produce. But once it's on the stair, it will require refinishing less frequently, a real consideration for a surface that sees as much use as a stair tread.

I prefer a satin gloss, both to reduce slipping and to enchance the wood grain without hiding it beneath a garish reflection. Treads should get three coats of varnish, all other surfaces two. To minimize the problem of treads and risers cupping, it's a good idea to seal the bottom of the stair too, with just as many coats as you give the top. In some cases, it may be easier to finish the parts ahead of assembly. Just be sure to leave the gluing surfaces free of finish. Balusters and railings are usually much easier to finish before they're installed.

Cove molding (facing page) gives the stair a finished look and hides minor gaps between the mitered skirt and the tread. Above, filler blocks inserted in the dado help anchor the tops of the balusters. They're intentionally thicker than the dado's depth and are chamfered along the edges.

Because of its steep rise, the ladder stair is ideal when floor space is acutely limited. This stair ascends into a loft in the author's shop.

An Open-Riser Ladder Stair

Chapter 6

In building stairs, you will occasionally encounter an instance where there's just not enough room for a comfortable rise and run, let alone one that meets the building code's ideal specs. An open-riser ladder stair is a good solution in such instances. Codes do not require stairs to unoccupied attics and lofts, so it's up to the local code inspector to approve a ladder that doesn't meet rise and run requirements. In instances where the ladder does connect occupied spaces, a commercially made alternating tread stair will meet code requirements.

As shown in the photo on the facing page, a ladder stair ascends steeply, so it requires very little floor space. This makes the ladder ideal for attic spaces or as a utility stair between a small basement and the main floor. It's obviously not a good choice for toddlers or for elderly folks. I'll use a ladder stair only as a last resort or as a secondary means of getting from one level to the next. Whenever practical, be sure to include a secure railing.

Besides taking up less floor space, a ladder stair's structure is open to view, allowing light and air to pass through it. This makes the stair look less imposing, so it appears to occupy even less space. In fact, some people like the open-riser design so much that they adapt it to a stair with conventional rise and run, opening up some interesting design possibilities, such as elegant hardwood carriages with through-mortised and wedged risers or carriages made of sectioned logs.

Design and construction methods

An open-riser ladder doesn't normally have cut carriages, although it could have if its ascent is shallow. The usual construction method is to fasten the treads directly to the carriages, similar to the housed-stringer method described in Chapter 4. However, instead of mortises and wedges, the treads are fastened using one of the methods shown in Figure 42 on p. 108. One of the simplest methods is the fully housed dado, a joint that runs from the front edge to the back edge of the carriage. This method could allow part of the tread to project beyond the front edge of the carriage, but a nicer touch is to stop the dado short of the front edge and then cut a shoulder on the tread, as shown in Figure 42.

At the opposite end of the difficulty spectrum are through mortises with tenons wedged with a contrasting wood or made to extend past the carriage so they can be decorated with a chamfer or carving. The mortises can be square to the treads or cut in a diamond shape to match the angle of the stair's incline. Another method is to pass a threaded rod through both carriages with nuts on the outsides of the carriages. Tightening up the nuts pulls the carriages together, locking the treads in place. It's not beautiful, but it works.

Whereas a conventionally pitched stair needs carriages at least 2x10 or 2x12, for a steep open-riser stair you can get by with carriages as narrow as 2x6. This is because the steeper the stair, the greater the angle between the tread and the carriage. It also means that the carriages are in compression rather than in tension, so they're less bouncy, and because they aren't notched to receive the treads they're stronger too.

The width of the stairs is limited only by the size of the tread material available. A full 1-in. thick tread can span 36 in., especially if it's oak rather than fir or pine. Longer treads should be thicker but you don't have to jump from 1 in. to 1½ in. Have your millwork shop plane your treads to 1¼ in. or whatever thickness seems structurally adequate without looking bulky.

Thickness is also a function of tread width. Obviously, a 2x4 can span less on the flat than a 2x10. A good test is simply to put a piece of tread on the floor, supported at either end by 2x4s spaced the same distance apart as the carriages. Stand on the tread and bounce a bit. If it feels

Figure 42: Tread Joinery

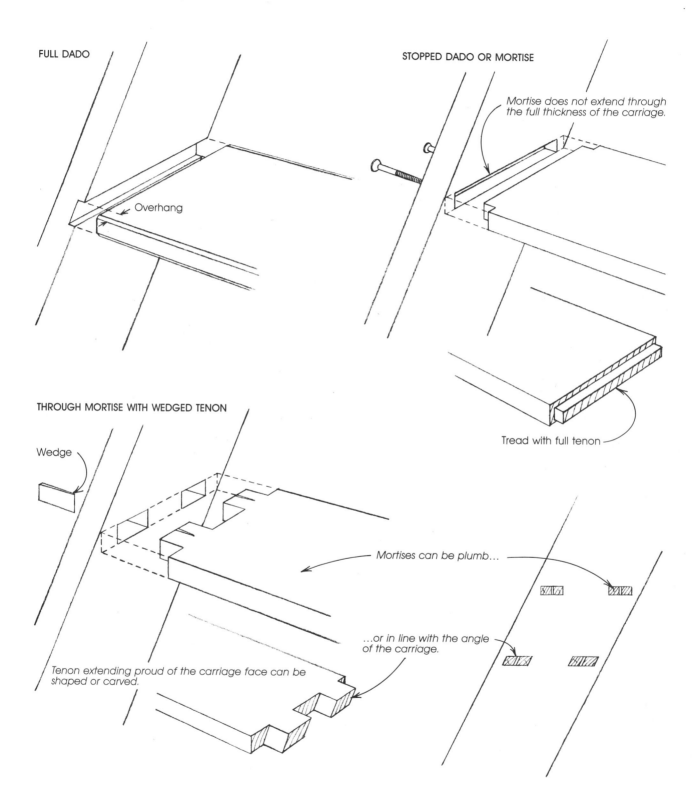

FULL DADO

Overhang

STOPPED DADO OR MORTISE

Mortise does not extend through the full thickness of the carriage.

Tread with full tenon

THROUGH MORTISE WITH WEDGED TENON

Wedge

Mortises can be plumb...

...or in line with the angle of the carriage.

Tenon extending proud of the carriage face can be shaped or carved.

To lay out the carriages, first put them in place and mark for the bottom level cut.

too bouncy, it's either too thin or the carriages are too far apart. Unless you've really guessed wrong, the tread isn't likely to break. The point is to make it feel solid.

Layout. I consider any stair with an incline greater than 45° to be a ladder stair (if the angle is greater than 75°, the stair is a plain ladder). In a ladder stair, the unit rise will vary between 9 in. and 12 in., larger than you'd tolerate in a conventional stair. The rise and run formulas described in Chapter 1 aren't practical, however, because the relationship of rise and run is inverted. In other words, there is more rise than run.

The simplest way to lay out the carriages is by the empirical method, using a story pole. Just stand one or both carriages (extra-long at this point) in the stairwell opening at an angle which fits the amount of space available for total run. Then mark the horizontal bottom cut with a level, as shown in the photo above. Saw the bottom cut, then put the carriage back in place to mark the vertical cut where it meets the framing or wall. When you have made this cut, put the carriage back in place and mark the level of the upper finish floor. The top cut can be flush with the finish floor or higher, depending on the design of the stairs. It's even possible to extend the car-

Mark the total rise on the story pole (above) and divide it by the number of treads to obtain unit rise. Using the story pole, mark unit rise on the carriages in place (right).

riages 30 in. or more above the upper floor to act as hand-rails, shipladder style.

To obtain the total vertical rise, simply place the story pole in the stairwell opening and mark the finish-floor to finish-floor dimension, as shown in the photo at left on the facing page. Divide this dimension by the number of treads you wish to use to arrive at the unit rise. If the rise is too high or too low, adjust the number of treads accordingly. In this stair, I used a unit rise of 11⅝ in.

You can mark these divisions on a story pole and lay out the carriages as shown in Figure 43, or use a tape measure and square or dividers, as described on pp. 34-37. You don't have to drop the carriage because the first layout line you drew in represents the top of the treads, and the mortising jig will be referenced to this line.

If you prefer a mathematical solution to an empirical approach, calculate a unit rise from the total rise and choose an appropriate unit run. One formula that works is: Unit run = 20 − ⅘ Unit rise. That is to say, if the unit rise is 9 in., the unit run will be about 8 in. However, 8 in. is not necessarily the tread width, because the treads in most ladder stairs overlap each other quite a bit. In a conventional stair, of course, the nosing overhangs the tread below it by only the thickness of the tread. Too much overhang on a conventional stair is likely to cause people to trip, but overhang generally isn't a problem on a steep stair because you ascend it just as you would a ladder. Of course, if you already know what the unit run will be, you can rearrange the formula to solve for the unit rise: Unit rise = 15 − ¾ Unit run.

Figure 43: Story-Pole Layout

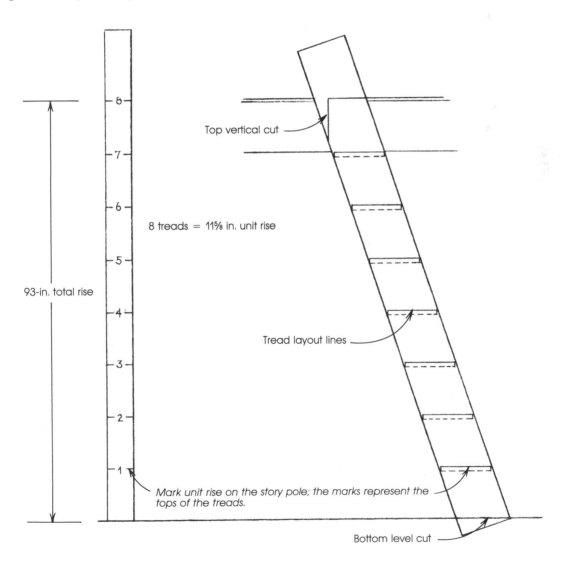

93-in. total rise

8 treads = 11⅝ in. unit rise

Top vertical cut

Tread layout lines

Mark unit rise on the story pole; the marks represent the tops of the treads.

Bottom level cut

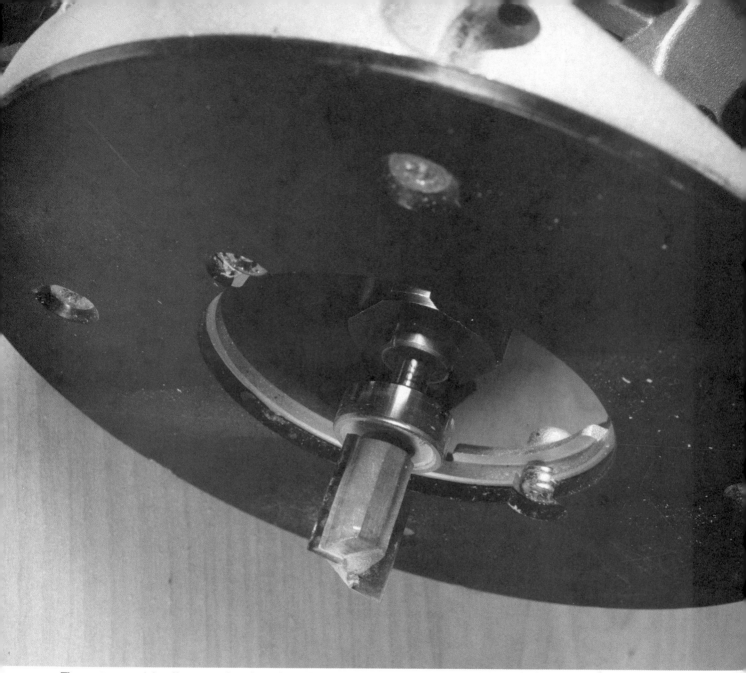

The router mortising jig uses a bearing whose diameter matches the bit's cutting diameter (above). Facing page: Fences tacked on either side of a tread set the dado width. The fences then guide the bearing to cut a slot in the jig base.

Tread joinery. For this stair, I've let the treads into dadoes, and for demonstration purposes, mortises routed in the carriages at the lowermost tread. As described in Figure 42 on p. 108, there are other ways to skin the cat, but any of them requiring mortises or dadoes can be done with the router jigs described here and on pp. 70-74.

The jigs can be any of three types: guided by the edge of the router, by a pilot bearing over or under the bit or by a guide bushing. In the photos, I'm using the bearing-over method. The jig shown here will fit only this tread thickness. You'd have to make another one for a stair with different treads. This jig is very direct. As shown in the photos on the facing page, simply tack to the jig base a pair of temporary fences around an actual piece of tread. Then, using these fences to guide the bearing, rout a slot in the jig base. Now remove the temporary fences, and the routed slot becomes the guide surface for the bearing. In actual use, clamp the jig to the carriage so that the top of the slot aligns with your layout lines. Rout the dadoes in several passes until you have achieved full depth.

On the bottom tread of the stair, I've demonstrated a stopped dado or mortise. This is made by tacking stop blocks at both ends of the jig. The ends of the mortises are rounded off by the router bit. You can either leave them round and shape the end of the tread to match, or you can square off the mortise with a chisel, which is what I did.

Making the treads. As with a conventional stair, the treads should first be ripped to width and then cut to length, allowing an extra 1 in. for the ½ in. the treads are let into the dadoes at each end. The treads for the ladder stair shown in this chapter are 8 in. wide and 30 in. long.

If possible, it's best to jig up your table saw or radial-arm saw for repeated accurate crosscuts. Any inconsistencies in the length of the treads or out-of-squareness will spoil the accuracy of the finished stair. This is especially true if you're cutting stop dadoes, because the shoulders at each end of the tread won't align if the tread ends aren't cut square.

Shoulders on the treads can be cut by hand or, more accurately, with a router setup or table saw and dado blade, as shown in the bottom photo on the facing page. For safety, make sure the tread clears the stop block clamped to the fence before it contacts the dado blade. Otherwise it could bind and kick back.

Facing page: Clamp the jig in place so that the top of the slot aligns with the layout lines, then rout the dado, moving the router from left to right when practical. To rout the mortises, tack stop blocks to the jig, as shown at left. Shoulder cuts on the treads can be cut with a dado blade on the table saw, as shown below.

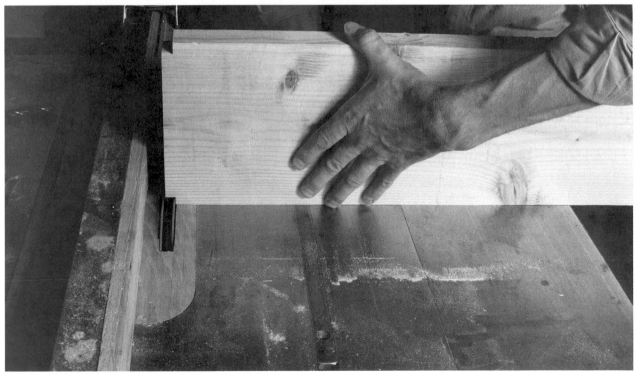

Square off the mortises with a chisel, as shown above, then try the fit (facing page).

If you are planning to make a full tenon on the ends of the treads (that is, one with four shoulders instead of two), a router rabbeting bit with a pilot does an accurate job of tenoning. The pilot bit automatically cuts the tenon to length, which can be ⅜ in. or ½ in., depending on the bit you use. The tenon thickness (which corresponds to the mortise width) is set with router depth. Since you will be cutting the tenon from both sides, set the cutting depth to a little less than ⅜ in. initially. In 1½-in. thick material, this depth will yield a tenon ¾ in. thick. Try the fit of the tenon, and then trim as necessary, removing a little material from both sides. Don't forget to adjust your dado jig to cut a mortise whose width is less than the thickness of the tread. As shown in the photo above, you'll have to chisel the dado or mortise corners square before fitting the treads.

Test-assemble the stair (above) and check it for square before screwing through the carriages and into the treads (facing page).

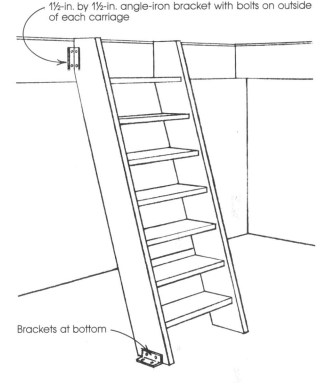

Figure 44: Carriage Fastening Methods

1½-in. by 1½-in. angle-iron bracket with bolts on outside of each carriage

Brackets at bottom

Assembly and installation

Unless the stairwell opening is too restrictive, a ladder stair is assembled first and then installed as a unit. Test-assemble the stair first to make sure all of the joints fit, and measure the carriages diagonally to check for square. Trim the joints as necessary to correct any problems. Before final assembly, sand both sides of the carriages and the treads. If you're building a fancy hardwood stair, you might consider finishing the parts before assembly. Just be certain not to get any varnish into the dadoes or on the tread ends; otherwise the glue won't stick. At final assembly, dab some glue into the mortises (for a hardwood stair), then clamp up the stair, checking for square once

again. Drive at least two 2½-in. screws through the carriages into the end grain of the treads.

Because a ladder stair is so steep, most of the load it bears is transmitted straight down. This means that you'll need good subfloor framing to avoid sagging, but the stair will have less tendency to kick out. It will need good anchoring, though it doesn't have to be as firmly attached as a conventional stair.

One way of attaching the top of a ladder to the framing is with brackets made from angle irons and bolts, as shown in Figure 44. A rough utility stair can be fastened with some simple sheet-metal angle clips and short nails. Brackets or even toenailing will do for fastening at the bottom of the ladder.

Further Reading

Alexander, Christopher et al. *A Pattern Language.* New York: Oxford University Press, 1977.

Anderson, L.O. and Taylor F. Winslow. *Wood-Frame House Construction.* Carlsbad, Calif.: Craftsman, 1976.

Badzinski, Stanley. *Stair Layout.* Homewood, Ill.: American Technical Publishers, 1971.

Feirer, John L. and Gilbert Hutchings. *Guide to Residential Carpentry.* New York: Charles Scribner's Sons, 1983.

Fine Homebuilding and *Fine Woodworking* magazines. The Taunton Press, 63 South Main Street, Box 5506, Newtown, Conn. 06470-5506.

Hop, Frederick U. *Design and Construction Techniques for the Residential Builder.* Englewood Cliffs, N. J.: Prentice-Hall, 1988.

"Installation Guide for Stairs," booklet, available at $2.50 from the L. J. Smith Stairway Co., 35280 Scio-Bowerston Road, Bowerston, Ohio 44695.

Love, T. W. *Stair Builders Handbook.* Carlsbad, Calif.: Craftsman, 1974.

Nash, George. *Old Houses: A Rebuilder's Manual.* Englewood Cliffs, N. J.: Prentice-Hall, 1979.

Syvanen, Bob. *Interior Finish.* Chester, Conn.: Globe-Pequot, 1982.

Index

Editor	Paul Bertorelli
Designer/layout artist	Ben Kann
Illustrators	Robert Goodfellow, Lynn McVicker
Art assistants	Jodie A. Delohery, Iliana Koehler
Copy editor	Peter Chapman
Production editor	Ruth Dobsevage
Typesetter	Lisa Carlson
Indexer	Harriet Hodges

Typeface	ITC Cheltenham Light